Modern Critical Interpretations

William Shakespeare's
A Midsummer Night's Dream

Modern Critical Interpretations

These and other titles in preparation

Modern Critical Interpretations

William Shakespeare's
A Midsummer Night's Dream

Edited and with an introduction by

Harold Bloom
Sterling Professor of the Humanities
Yale University

Chelsea House Publishers ◊

NEW YORK ◊ PHILADELPHIA

Library of Congress Cataloging-in-Publication Data

William Shakespeare's A midsummer night's dream.

   (Modern critical interpretations)
   Bibliography: p.
   Includes index.
   1. Shakespeare, William, 1564–1616.   Midsummer
night's dream.   I. Bloom, Harold.   II. Series.
PR2827.W54   1987   822.3'3   86-34328
ISBN 0-87754-933-8

Contents

Editor's Note

This book gathers together a representative selection of the most useful criticism of Shakespeare's *A Midsummer Night's Dream*, arranged in the chronological order of the critical essays' original publication. I am grateful to Susan Lasher for her aid in researching this volume.

My introduction centers upon Bottom and Puck as the antithetical figures at the two limits of the drama's vision. Anne Barton begins the chronological sequence of criticism with her study of the play's extraordinary adroitness in fusing materials of the utmost diversity. A very different mode of interpretation follows in René Girard's saturnine account of mimetic desire and self-deceit in the loves of Hermia, Helena, Lysander, and Demetrius.

Alvin B. Kernan provides a corrective to Girard's atemporal view by emphasizing the Elizabethan conventions that regulate the relations between actors and audience in *A Midsummer Night's Dream*. Comic transformations in the play are studied imagistically by Ruth Nevo, and rather more darkly by Jan Kott, for whom the play is orgiastic, almost a ritual of bestiality. A gentler perspective, deeply informed by contemporary feminism and its idealisms, is provided by David Marshall in his reading of the drama as a ritual of sexual exchange.

In this volume's final essay, the great Canadian critic Northrop Frye gives us a magisterial overview of the play, one that shows us the affinities of the wood-world with that part of the mind "below the reason's encounter with objective reality, and yet connected with the hidden creative powers of the mind."

Introduction

On the loftiest of the world's thrones we still are sitting only on our own Bottom.

MONTAIGNE, "Of Experience"

I will get Peter Quince to write a ballet of this dream. It shall be call'd "Bottom's Dream," because it hath no bottom.

I

I wish Shakespeare had given us Peter Quince's ballet (ballad), but he may have been too wise to attempt the poem. *A Midsummer Night's Dream*, for me, is Puck and Bottom, and I prefer Bottom. Perhaps we reduce to Puckish individuals or Bottoms. Pucks are more charming, but Bottoms are rather more amiable. Shakespeare's Bottom is surpassingly amiable, and I agree with Northrop Frye that Bottom is the only mortal with experience of the visionary center of the play. As the possible lover (however briefly) of the Fairy Queen, Bottom remains a lasting reproach to our contemporary fashion of importing sacred violence, bestiality, and all manner of sexual antics into Shakespeare's most fragile of visionary dramas. For who could be more mild mannered, better natured, or sweetly humorous than the unfailingly gentle Bottom? Titania ends up despising him, but he is simply too good for her!

Bottom, when we first encounter him, is already a Malaprop, inaccurate at the circumference, as it were, but sound at the core, which is what his name means, the center of the skein upon which a weaver's wool is wound. And surely that is his function in the play; he is its core, and also he is the most original figure in *A Midsummer Night's Dream*. Self-assertive, silly, ignorant, he remains a personage of absolute good will, a kind of remote ancestor to Joyce's amiable Poldy. Transformed into an outward monstrosity by Puck, he yet retains his

1

courage, kindness, and humor, and goes through his uncanny experience totally unchanged within. His initial dialogue with Titania is deliciously ironic, and he himself is in full control of the irony:

> TITANIA: I pray thee, gentle mortal, sing again.
>   Mine ear is much enamored of thy note;
>   So is mine eye enthralled to thy shape;
>   And thy fair virtue's force (perforce) doth move me
>   On the first view to say, to swear, I love thee.
> BOTTOM: Methinks, mistress, you should have little reason
>   for that. And yet, to say the truth, reason and love keep
>   little company together now-a-days. The more the pity
>   that some honest neighbors will not make them friends.
>   Nay, I can gleek upon occasion.
> TITANIA: Thou art as wise as thou art beautiful.
> BOTTOM: Not so, neither; but if I had wit enough to get out
>   of this wood, I have enough to serve mine own turn.

Knowing that he lacks both beauty and wisdom, Bottom is realistic enough to see that the faery queen is beautiful but not wise. Charmed by (and charming to) the elve foursome of Peaseblossom, Cobweb, Moth, and Mustardseed, Bottom makes us aware that they mean no more and no less to him than Titania does. Whether or not he has made love to Titania, a subject of some nasty debate among our critical contemporaries, seems to me quite irrelevant. What does matter is that he is sublimely unchanged, for worse or for better, when he wakes up from his bottomless dream:

> BOTTOM: [*Awaking.*] When my cue comes, call me, and I
>   will answer. My next is, "Most fair Pyramus." Heigh-ho!
>   Peter Quince! Flute the bellowsmender! Snout the tin-
>   ker! Starveling! God's my life, stol'n hence, and left me
>   asleep! I have had a most rare vision. I have had a
>   dream, past the wit of man to say what dream it was.
>   Man is but an ass, if he go about [t'] expound this
>   dream. Methought I was—there is no man can tell
>   what. Methought I was, and methought I had—but
>   man is but [a patch'd] fool, if he will offer to say what
>   methought I had. The eye of man hath not heard, the
>   ear of man hath not seen, man's hand is not able to
>   taste, his tongue to conceive, nor his heart to report,

what my dream was. I will get Peter Quince to write a
ballet of this dream. It shall be call'd "Bottom's Dream,"
because it hath no bottom; and I will sing it in the latter
end of a play, before the Duke. Peradventure, to make
it the more gracious, I shall sing it at her death.

Bottom's revision of 1 Corinthians 2:9–10 is the heart of the
matter:

Eye hath not seen, nor ear heard, neither have entered into
the heart of man, the things which God hath prepared for
them that love him.

But God hath revealed them unto us by his Spirit.

(St. Paul)

The eye of man hath not heard, the ear of man hath not
seen, man's hand is not able to taste, his tongue to conceive,
nor his heart to report, what my dream was.

(Bottom)

Bottom's scrambling of the senses refuses St. Paul's easy supernat-
uralism, with its dualistic split between flesh and spirit. Our prophet
Bottom is a monist, and so his dream urges upon us a synesthetic
reality, fusing flesh and spirit. That Bottom is one for whom God has
prepared the things revealed by his Spirit is made wonderfully clear in
the closing dialogue between the benign weaver and Theseus:

BOTTOM: [*Starting up.*] No, I assure you, the wall is down
that parted their fathers. Will it please you to see the
epilogue, or to hear a Bergomask dance between two of
our company?
THESEUS: No epilogue, I pray you; for your play needs no
excuse.

Only Bottom could assure us that the wall is down that parted all our
fathers. The weaver's common sense and natural goodness bestow
upon him an aesthetic dignity, homely and humane, that is the necessary counterpoise to the world of Puck that otherwise would ravish
reality away in Shakespeare's visionary drama.

II

Puck, being the spirit of mischief, is both a hobgoblin and "sweet Puck," not so much by turns but all at once. *A Midsummer Night's Dream* is more Puck's play than Bottom's, I would reluctantly agree, even as *The Tempest* is more Ariel's drama than it is poor Caliban's. If Puck, rather than Oberon, were in charge, then Bottom never would resume human shape and the four young lovers would continue their misadventures forever. Most of what fascinates our contemporaries about *A Midsummer Night's Dream* belongs to Puck's vision rather than to Bottom's. Amidst so much of the Sublime, it is difficult to prefer any single passage, but I find most unforgettable Puck's penultimate chant:

> Now the hungry [lion] roars,
> And the wolf [behowls] the moon;
> Whilst the heavy ploughman snores,
> All with weary task foredone.
> Now the wasted brands do glow,
> Whilst the screech-owl, screeching loud,
> Puts the wretch that lies in woe
> In remembrance of a shroud.
> Now it is the time of night
> That the graves, all gaping wide,
> Every one lets forth his sprite,
> In the church-way paths to glide.
> And we fairies, that do run
> By the triple Hecat's team
> From the presence of the sun,
> Following darkness like a dream,
> Now are frolic. Not a mouse
> Shall disturb this hallowed house.
> I am sent with broom before,
> To sweep the dust behind the door.

Everything problematic about Puck is summed up there; a domestic, work-a-day spirit, yet always uncannily *between*, between men and women, faeries and humans, nobles and mechanicals, nature and art, space and time. Puck is a spirit cheerfully amoral, free because never in love, and always more amused even than amusing. The triple Hecate—heavenly moon maiden, earthly Artemis, and ruler of Hades—is more especially Puck's deity than she is the goddess worshipped by the other faeries. Hazlitt wisely contrasted Puck to Ariel by reminding us that "Ariel is a minister of retribution, who is touched with the sense of pity at the woes he inflicts," while Puck "laughs at those whom he misleads." Puck just does not care; he has nothing to gain and little to lose. Only Oberon could call him "gentle," but then Oberon could see Cupid flying between moon and earth, and Puck constitutionally could not. Puck says that things please him best "that befall preposterously,"; where I think the last word takes on the force of the later coming earlier and the earlier later. As a kind of flying metalepsis or trope of transumption, Puck is indeed what the rhetorician Puttenham called a far-fetcher.

The midsummer night's dream, Puck tells us in his final chant, is ours, since we "but slumb'red here, / While these visions did appear." What are we dreaming when we dream Puck? "Shadows" would be his reply, in a familiar Shakespearean trope, yet Puck is no more a shadow than Bottom is. Free of love, Puck becomes an agent of the irrational element in love, its tendency to over-value the object, as Freud grimly phrased it. A man or woman who incarnates Puck is sexually very dangerous, because he or she is endlessly mobile, invariably capable of transforming object-libido back into ego-libido again. Puckish freedom is overwhelmingly attractive, but the blow it strikes you will cause it no pain. Falling in love with a Puck is rather like turning life into the game of hockey.

Theseus, in the play's most famous speech, associates the lover with the poet and the lunatic in a perfectly Freudian conglomerate, since all forsake the reality principle, all assert the omnipotence of thought, and all thus yield themselves up to an ultimate narcissism. If Theseus is a Freudian, Bottom is not, but represents an older wisdom, the amiable sapience, mixed with silliness, of the all-too-natural man. Puck, quicksilver and uncaring, defines the limits of the human by being so far apart from the human.

How can one play contain both Bottom and Puck? Ariel and Caliban both care, though they care on different sides and in different modes. Puck has no human feelings, and so no human meaning; Bottom is one of the prime Shakespearean instances of how human meaning gets started, by a kind of immanent overflow, an ontological excess of being in excess of language. Only a dream, we might think, could contain both Bottom and Puck, but the play, however fantastic, is no fantasy, but an imitation that startles the reality principle and makes it tremble, rather like a guilty thing surprised.

The Synthesizing Impulse
of *A Midsummer Night's Dream*

Anne Barton

A Midsummer Night's Dream was first printed in a quarto edition in
1600. The comedy was first mentioned by Meres in 1598, but 1595–96
is usually accepted as the date of composition. It has certain stylistic
affinities with *Richard II* and *Romeo and Juliet,* plays which must have
been written at about the same time. More importantly, it seems to
consolidate and conclude Shakespeare's first period of experiment with
comic form. The synthesizing impulse characteristic of *A Midsummer
Night's Dream* not only knits together a number of different historical
times and places, literary traditions, character types, and modes of
thought. It manifests itself in the play's unusual variety of metres and
verse forms, as well as in the tendency, remarked on by several critics,
for characters to stress the richness of their encompassing dramatic
world by listing its components. Egeus is not content simply to state
that Lysander has exchanged love-tokens with Hermia. He names
them all: "bracelets of thy hair, rings, gawds, conceits, / Knacks,
trifles, nosegays, sweetmeats" (1.1.33–34). Almost all the characters
are given to list-making. Oberon painstakingly itemizes every kind of
wild beast that might conceivably wake Titania; Hermia and Lysander
count all the obstacles that have ever threatened true love, while the
fairies almost bury Bottom alive under a deluge of honey and butter-
flies, glow-worms, apricots and figs.

Shakespeare's friend Ben Jonson was, in many of his plays, a compulsive maker of dramatic inventories of a superficially similar kind. *Volpone, The Alchemist* and *Bartholomew Fair* are filled with tallies, a sea of objects which continually threaten to engulf the characters. Nothing, however, could be more different in effect from the list-making of *A Midsummer Night's Dream*. Jonson's world of things is stifling and corrupt, inanimate, man-made and man-soiled, the dusty contents of some Gothic lumber-room of the imagination: "his copper rings, / His saffron jewel, with the toad-stone in't, / Or his embroidered suit, with the cope-stitch, / Made of a hearse-cloth, or his old tilt-feather" (*Volpone*, 2.5.11–14). Almost invariably, Jonson's enumerations evoke an incoherent urban world, so overcrowded that it has become impossible for human beings to walk about naturally among the detritus of a civilization out of control. By contrast, the lists in Shakespeare's comedy create the sense of a country world that is inexhaustibly rich and various, occasionally grotesque, but basically fresh, creative, and young. Moreover, where Jonson's lists are deliberately disjunctive, images of chaos, Shakespeare's relate and interact without sacrificing the individuality of the separate components. In the remarkably generous and inclusive order of *A Midsummer Night's Dream,* where Bottom can converse amiably with the fairy queen without losing a jot of his own identity, there seems to be nothing which the shaping spirit of imagination cannot use and, in some way, make relevant to the whole.

Not surprisingly, a preoccupation with the idea of imagination, and with some of its products—dreams, the illusions of love, poetry and plays—is central to this comedy. Theseus may speak somewhat slightingly of "the lunatic, the lover, and the poet," beings "of imagination all compact" whose fantasies are literally incredible: "more strange than true" (5.1.2). The play as a whole takes a far more complicated view of the matter. Theseus himself, for Shakespeare as for Chaucer and Sophocles, is preeminently the hero of a daylight world of practicalities, of the active as opposed to the contemplative life. His relationship with Hippolyta in the comedy presents an image of passion steadied by the relative maturity of the people involved. There are ages of love as well as of human life and Theseus and Hippolyta represent summer as opposed to the giddy spring fancies of the couples lost in the wood. Theseus is a wise ruler and a good man, but Shakespeare makes it plain that there are other, important areas of human experience with which he is incompetent to deal. When Theseus leads the bridal couples to bed at the end of act 5 with the mocking reminder that " 'tis almost fairy time" (5.1.364), he intends the remark as a last jibe at Hermia and Lysander, Helena and Demetrius: people who, in his estimation, have been led all too easily by darkness and their own fear to suppose a bush a bear (5.1.22). The joke, however, is on Theseus. It is indeed almost fairy time. In fact, Puck, Oberon, and Titania have been waiting for this moment in order to take over the palace. For a few nocturnal hours the wood infiltrates the urban world. Even so, years before, a Titania in whom Theseus apparently does not believe led him "through the glimmering night / From Perigenia, whom he ravished," and made him "with fair Aegles break his faith, / With Ariadne, and Antiopa" (2.1.77–80). The life of the self-appointed critic of imagination and the irrational is permeated by exactly those qualities he is concerned to minimize or reject. Gently, the comedy suggests that while it is certainly possible to mistake a bush for a bear, one may also err as Theseus does by confounding a genuine bear with a bush. The second mistake is, on the whole, the more dangerous.

The last act of *A Midsummer Night's Dream* is concerned principally, and even somewhat self-consciously, with the relationship between art and life, dreams and the waking world. In terms of plot, this fifth act is superfluous. Almost all the business of the comedy has been concluded at the end of act 4: the error of Titania's vision put right and she herself reconciled with Oberon, Hermia paired off happily with Lysander and Helena with Demetrius. Theseus has not only overruled the objections of old Egeus, but insisted upon associating these marriages with his own: "Away with us to Athens. Three and three / We'll hold a feast in great solemnity" (4.1.184–85). This couplet has the authentic ring of a comedy conclusion. Only one expectation generated by the action remains unfulfilled: the presentation of the Pyramus and Thisby play before the Duke and his bride. Out of this single remaining bit of material, Shakespeare constructs a fifth act which seems, in effect, to take place beyond the normal, plot-defined boundaries of comedy.

The new social order which has emerged from the ordeal of the wood makes its first public appearance at the performance of the mechanicals' play. It is sensitive and hopeful. Theseus, characteristically, is condescending about the actor's art: "The best in this kind are but shadows; and the worst are no worse, if imagination amend them" (5.1.211–12). Richard Burbage would scarcely have thanked him. Such a view of the theatre overstresses the audience's lordly willingness-to-be-fooled at the expense of the power of illusion. Certainly a quite extraordinary effort of imagination would be required to extract

Aristotelian pity and fear from the tragedy of Pyramus and Thisby as enacted by Bottom and Flute. The courtly audience, like the theatre audience, laughs at the ineptitudes and absurdities of the play within the play. Unlike Berowne and his friends in the equivalent scene of *Love's Labor's Lost*, however, the on-stage spectators in *A Midsummer Night's Dream* remain courteous. Most of the remarks made by Theseus, Hippolyta, and the four lovers are not heard by the preoccupied actors. Those that do penetrate, suggestions as to the proper disposition of Moonshine's lantern, dog, and bush, cries of "Well roar'd, Lion" and "Well run, Thisby," are entirely in the spirit of the performance. It was Bottom, after all, back in the rehearsal stage, who fondly imagined a success for Lion so great that the audience would intervene to request an encore: "Let him roar again." Gratifyingly, this wish-dream just about comes true. As the play proceeds, tolerance ripens into geniality, into an unforced accord between actors and spectators based upon considerations far more complex than anything articulated by Theseus. Although the artistic merit of the Pyramus and Thisby play is virtually non-existent, the performance itself is a resounding success. No feelings have been hurt, and everyone has had a thoroughly good time. Even Theseus finds that "this palpable-gross play hath well beguil'd / The heavy gait of night" (5.1.367–68).

For the theatre audience, granted a perspective wider than the one enjoyed by Theseus and the members of his court, the Pyramus and Thisby story of love thwarted by parents and the enmity of the stars consolidates and in a sense defines the happy ending of *A Midsummer Night's Dream*. It reminds us of the initial dilemma of Hermia and Lysander, and also of how their story might well have ended: with blood and deprivation. The heavy rhetoric of the interlude fairly bristles with fate and disaster, introducing into act 5 a massing of images of death. The entire action of the play within the play is tragic in intention, although not in execution. Without meaning to do so, Bottom and his associates transform tragedy into farce before our eyes, converting that litany of true love crossed which was rehearsed in the very first scene by Hermia and Lysander to laughter. In doing so, they recapitulate the development of *A Midsummer Night's Dream* as a whole, reenacting its movement from potential calamity to an ending in which quick bright things come not to confusion, as once seemed inevitable, but to joy. An intelligent director can and should ensure that the on-stage audience demonstrates some awareness of the ground-bass of mortality sounding underneath the hilarity generated by Bottom's performance, that a line like Lysander's "he is dead, he is nothing" (5.1.308–9) is not lost in the merriment. Only the theatre audience, however, can capture the full resonance of the Pyramus and Thisby play.

When Theseus dismisses the actors after the Bergomask, and the members of the stage audience depart to their chambers, *A Midsummer Night's Dream* seems once again to have arrived at its ending. For the second time Theseus is given a couplet which sounds like the last lines of a play (5.1.369–70). When something like this happened at the end of act 4 it was Bottom, starting up out of his sleep, who set the comedy going again. This time it is the entrance of the fairies, but again the prolongation has nothing to do with plot. The appearance of Puck, Oberon, Titania and their train in the heart of Athens lends a symmetry to the action which would otherwise have been lacking and also gives the lie to Theseus's scepticism. Most important of all, however, is the way Puck's speech picks up and transforms precisely those ideas of death and destruction distanced through laughter in the Pyramus and Thisby play.

> Now the hungry lion roars,
> And the wolf behowls the moon;
> Whilst the heavy ploughman snores,
> All with weary task foredone.
> Now the wasted brands do glow,
> Whilst the screech-owl, screeching loud,
> Puts the wretch that lies in woe
> In remembrance of a shroud.
> Now it is the time of night
> That the graves, all gaping wide,
> Every one lets forth his sprite,
> In the church-way paths to glide.

All the images here are of sickness, toil, and death. Even the wasted brands, in context, suggest the inevitable running down of human life as it approaches the grave.

Once again, Shakespeare has adjusted the balance between art and life, reality and illusion. Puck's hungry lion is something genuinely savage, not at all the "very gentle beast, and of a good conscience" (5.1.227–28) impersonated by Snug. Even so, his talk of graves and shrouds, drudgery and exhaustion, brings the sense of mortality kept at bay in the Pyramus and Thisby interlude closer, preparing us for the true end of the comedy after so many feints and false conclusions. Puck's speech begins a modulation which will terminate, some fifty lines later, in direct address to the audience and in a player's request for applause. Actors and spectators alike will be turned out of Athens to face the workaday world. Yet Shakespeare refuses to concede that Theseus was right. In the first place, Puck's account of the terrors of the night is not final. It serves to introduce Oberon and Titania, the most fantastic characters in the play, and in their hands Puck's night fears turn into benediction and blessing. About the facts of mortality themselves the fairy king and queen can do nothing, even as Titania could do nothing to prevent the death, years before, of the votaress of her order. All they can do is to strengthen the fidelity and trust of the three pairs of lovers, to bless these marriages, and to stress the positive side of the night as a time for love and procreation as well as for death and fear. Certainly the emphasis on the fair, unblemished children to be born is not accidental, something to be explained purely in terms of the possible occasion of the play's first performance. These children summoned up by Oberon extend the comedy into the future, counteracting the artificial finality which always threatens to diminish happy endings. A beginning is made implicit in the final moments of the play, a further and wider circle.

Unlike characters in fairy-tale, Theseus and Hippolyta, Demetrius and Helena, Lysander and Hermia cannot live happily ever after. Only the qualified immortality to be obtained through offspring is available to them. It was an idea of survival in time which the Shakespeare of the sonnets came to distrust. Nevertheless, in the general atmosphere of celebration and blessing at the end of *A Midsummer Night's Dream*, it seems for the moment enough. It is only after this final coming together in Theseus's palace of the two poles of the comedy, a world of fantasy and one of fact, of immortality and of death, that Puck turns to speak to the theatre audience. Like Theseus, he describes the actors as "shadows" and sums up the play now concluded as a "weak and idle theme, / No more yielding than a dream." When John Lyly ended his court comedies with superficially similar words of deprecation and apology, he seems to have meant them literally. Shakespeare is far more devious. Images of sleep and dreams, shadows and illusions, have been used so constantly in the course of the comedy, examined and invested with such body and significance that they cannot be regarded now as simple terms of denigration and dismissal. As with that mock-apology for the author's "rough and all-unable pen" which concludes *Henry V*, Shakespeare seems to have felt able to trust his audience to take the point: to recognize the simplification, and to understand that the play has created its own reality, a reality touching our own at every point which

> More witnesseth than fancy's images,
> And grows to something of great constancy;
> But howsoever, strange and admirable.
>
> (5.1.25–27)

Myth and Ritual in Shakespeare: A Midsummer Night's Dream

René Girard

> I have *considered, our whole life is like a* Play: *wherein every man, forgetfull*
> *of himselfe, is in travaile with expression of another. Nay, wee so insist*
> *in imitating others, as wee cannot (when it is necessary) returne to ourselves;*
> *like Children, that imitate the vices of* Stammerers *so long, till at last*
> *they become such; and make the habit to another nature, as it is never forgotten.*
> BEN JONSON, Timber of Discoveries

The opening scene of *A Midsummer Night's Dream* leads the audience to
expect an ordinary comedy plot. Boy and girl love each other. A mean
old father is trying to separate them, with the help of the highest
authority in the land, Theseus, duke of Athens. Unless she gives up
Lysander, Hermia will have no choice but death or the traditional
convent. As soon as this formidable edict is proclaimed, the father
figures depart, leaving the lovers to their own devices. They launch
into a duet on the impediments of love: age difference, social conditions, and, last but not least, coercion by those in authority.

The two victimized youngsters leisurely and chattingly prepare to
flee their ferocious tyrants; they plunge into the woods; Hermia is
pursued by Demetrius, himself pursued by Helena, Hermia's best
friend, whom, of course, he spurns. The first couple's happiness appears threatened from the outside, but the second couple, even from
the start, insist on being unhappy by themselves, always falling in love
with the wrong person. We soon realize that Shakespeare is more
interested in this systematically self-defeating type of passion than in

From *Textual Strategies: Perspectives in Post-Structuralist Criticism*, edited by Josué
V. Harari. © 1979 by Cornell University. Cornell University Press, 1979.

15

the initial theme of "true love," something unconquerable by definition and always in need of villainous enemies if it is to provide any
semblance of dramatic plot.

It quickly turns out that self-defeating passion dominates the relationship of not just one but both couples, involving them in a fourway
merry-go-round that never seems to allow any amorous reciprocity
even though partners are continually exchanged. At first the two
young men are in love with Hermia; then, during the night, both
abandon that girl and fall in love with the other. The only constant
element in the configuration is the convergence of more than one
desire on a single object, as if perpetual rivalries were more important
to the four characters than their changing pretexts.

Although the theme of outside interference is not forgotten, it
becomes even more flimsy. In the absence of the father figures, the
role is entrusted to Puck, who keeps pouring his magical love juice
into the "wrong" eyes. When Oberon rebukes Puck for his mistake,
he does so with a show of emotion, in a precipitous monologue that
ironically reflects the confusion it pretends to clear, thereby casting
doubt upon the reality of the distinctions it pretends to restore:

> What hast thou done? Thou hast mistaken quite,
> And laid the love juice on some true love's sight:
> Of thy misprision must perforce ensue
> Some true love turned, and not a false turned true.
>
> (3.2.88–91)

Who will tell the difference between *some true love turned* and *a false
turned true*? We may suspect a more serious rationale for the four
protagonists' miseries, for the growing hysteria of the midsummer
night. A close look reveals something quite systematic about the
behavior of the four, underlined by more than a few ironic suggestions. The author is hinting at something which is never made fully
explicit, but which seems cogent and coherent enough to call for a
precise formulation.

The midsummer night is a process of increasing violence. Demetrius
and Lysander end up in a duel; the violence of the girls' rivalry almost
matches that of the boys. Their fierce quarreling certainly contradicts—or
does it?—Helena's earlier expression of unbounded admiration for her
friend Hermia:

> Your eyes are lodestars, and your tongue's sweet air,
> More tunable than lark to shepherd's ear,

When wheat is green, when hawthorn buds appear.
Sickness is catching. O! were favor so,
Yours would I catch, fair Hermia, ere I go;
My ear should catch your voice, my eye your eye,
My tongue should catch your tongue's sweet melody.
Were the world mine, Demetrius being bated,
The rest I'd give to be to you translated.

(1.1.183–91)

This is a strange mixture of quasi-religious and yet sensuous worship. The last line admirably sums up the significance of the passage. Desire speaks here, and it is desire for another's *being*. Helena would like to be *translated,* metamorphosed into Hermia, because Hermia enjoys the love of Demetrius. Demetrius, however, is hardly mentioned. The desire for him appears less pressing than the desire for Hermia's being. In that desire, what truly stands out is the irresistible sexual dominance that Hermia is supposed to exert upon Demetrius and all those who approach her. It is this sexual dominance that Helena envies: "O teach me how you look and with what art / You sway the motion of Demetrius' heart" (1.1.192–93). Helena sees Hermia as the magnetic pole of desires in their common little world, and she would like to be that. The other three characters are no different; they all worship the same erotic absolute, the same ideal image of seduction which each girl and boy in turn appears to embody in the eyes of the others. This absolute has nothing to do with concrete qualities; it is properly metaphysical. Even though obsessed with the flesh, desire is divorced from it; it is not instinctive and spontaneous; it never seems to know directly and immediately where its object lies; in order to locate that object, it cannot rely on such things as the pleasure of the eyes and the other senses. In its perpetual *noche oscura,* metaphysical desire must therefore trust in another and supposedly more enlightened desire on which it patterns itself. As a consequence, desire, in *A Midsummer Night's Dream*, perpetually runs to desire just as money runs to money in the capitalistic system. We may, say, of course, that the four characters are in love with love. That would not be inaccurate; but there is no such thing as love or desire in general, and such a formulation obscures the most crucial point, the necessarily jealous and conflictual nature of mimetic convergence on a single object. If we keep borrowing each other's desires, if we allow our respective desires to agree on the same object, we, as individuals, are bound to disagree.

The erotic absolute will inevitably be embodied in a successful rival. Helena cannot fail to be torn between worship and hatred of Hermia. Imitative desire makes all reciprocal rapports impossible. Shakespeare makes this point very clear, but for some reason no one wants to hear. The audience resembles the lovers themselves, who talk ceaselessly about "true love" but obviously do not care to understand the mechanism of their own feelings.

Metaphysical desire is mimetic, and mimetic desire cannot be let loose without breeding a midsummer night of jealousy and strife. Yet the protagonists never feel responsible for the state of their affairs; they never hesitate to place the blame where it does not belong, on an unfavorable fate, on reactionary parents, on mischievous fairies, and on other such causes. Throughout the play, the theme of outside interference provides much of the obvious dramatic structure; and we must suspect that it is not simply juxtaposed to the midsummer night which, in a sense, it contradicts: the two may well be in a more complex relationship of disguise and reality, never clearly spelled out and formalized, allowing enough juxtaposition and imbrication so that the play, at least in some important respects, can really function as two plays at once. On one level it is a traditional comedy, destined for courtly audiences and their modern successors; but, underneath, mimetic desire holds sway, responsible not only for the delirium and frenzy of the midsummer night but also for all the mythical themes which reign supreme at the upper level.

The real obstacles are not outside the enchanted circle of the lovers: each of them is an obstacle to the others in a game of imitation and rivalry that is their mode of alienation, and this alienation finally verges on trancelike possession. The outside obstacle is an illusion, often a transparent one, a telltale disguise of the real situation, constructed so that it can serve as an allegory. It even happens that absolutely nothing has to be changed in order to pass from the truth to the lie and back again to the truth: the same words mean both the one and the other. Shakespeare loves to play on these ambiguities. I have already mentioned the love duet between Lysander and Hermia: most critics would agree that it constitutes a parody of fashionable clichés, and they are no doubt correct; but we cannot view this parodic character as sufficient justification in itself. The real purpose cannot be parody for parody's sake. There must be something more, something which Shakespeare definitely wants to say and which we are likely to miss because it will appear in the form of "rhetoric." In the duet part of that love scene, the first seven lines seem to mark a gradation which leads up to the eighth, on which the emphasis falls:

LYSANDER: The course of true love never did run smooth;
But either it was different in blood—
HERMIA: O cross! Too high to be enthralled to low.
LYSANDER: Or else misgraffed in respect of years—
HERMIA: O spite! Too old to be engaged to young.
LYSANDER: Or else it stood upon the choice of friends—
HERMIA: O hell! To choose love by another's eyes.

(1.1.134–40)

The last two lines can be read as only one more "cross," the most relevant really, the one we would expect to see mentioned first in the present context. The reference to "friends" is somewhat unexpected, but not so strange as to merit a second thought for most listeners. But if we isolate these last two lines, if we replace the love mystique in the spirit of which they are uttered with the present context, the context of the preceding remarks and of countless Shakespearean scenes (not only in *A Midsummer Night's Dream* but also in almost every other play), another meaning will appear, a meaning more evident and infinitely more significant.

Everywhere in Shakespeare there is a passion which is primarily the copy of a model, a passion that is destructive not only because of its sterile rivalries but because it dissolves reality: it tends to the abstract, the merely representational. The model may be present in the flesh and strut on the stage of the theater; and it may also rise from the pages of a book, come out of the frame of a picture, turn into the worship of a phantom, verbal or iconic. The model is always a text. It is Othello's heroic language, the real object of fascination for Desdemona rather than Othello himself. It is the portrait of Portia which her lover chooses to contemplate in preference to the original. This metaphysical passion is a corruption of life, always open to the corruptive suggestions of mediators and go-betweens, such as the Pandarus of *Troilus and Cressida*. The paramount role that Shakespeare attributes to such desire, in an obviously calculated way, even in relationships where we may least expect it, is matched only in the works of such writers as Cervantes, Molière, or Dostoevsky. *O hell! To choose love by another's eyes.* Since the phrase is uttered in conformity with the ideology of "true love," surely appropriate to a royal wedding (the occasion of *A Midsummer Night's Dream*), the true Shakespearean meaning must dawn upon us, prompted not only by the events that follow but by a thousand echoes from all the other plays.

Mimetic desire remains unperceived even when it is most obvious. In the very process of being denied, displaced, reified, it still manages to proclaim its own truth. Almost every time they open their mouths, the lovers unwittingly proclaim what at the same time they ignore, and we generally go in ignoring it along with them. The midsummer night is a hell of the lovers' own choosing, a hell into which they all avidly plunge, insofar as they all choose to choose love by another's eyes. Hermia, talking about the turn her love affair with Lysander has given her own life, naively recognizes that the hell is all hers, and that it was already there before the appearance of the parental and supernatural bugaboos that are supposed to be its cause:

> Before the time I did Lysander see,
> Seemed Athens as a paradise to me.
> O then, what graces in my love do dwell,
> That he hath turned a heaven into a hell!
>
> (1.1.204–7)

Shakespeare is making fun of us, of course. He seems intent on proving that you can say almost anything in a play as long as you provide the audience with the habitual props of comedy, the conventional expressions of "true love," even in minimal amounts, adding, of course, a ferocious father figure or two to satisfy the eternal Freudian in us. As long as the standard plot is vaguely outlined, even in the crudest and least believable fashion, the author can subvert his own myths and state the truth at every turn, with no consequences whatsoever. The audience will instinctively and automatically rally around the old clichés, so completely blind and deaf to everything which may contradict them that the presence of this truth will not even be noticed. The continued misunderstanding of the play throughout the centuries gives added resonance to the point Shakespeare is secretly making, providing ironic confirmation that the most worn-out myth will always triumph over the most explicit demythification.

If the subject persists in his self-defeating path, the rivalries into which mimetic desire inevitably runs must logically be viewed as glorious signs and heralds of the absolute that keeps eluding him. Mimetic desire breeds rejection and failure; it is rejection and failure that it must ultimately seek. The impossible is always preferred to the possible, the unreal to the real, the hostile and unwilling to the willing and available. This self-destructive character flows directly and auto-matically from the mechanical consequences of the first definition: *to choose love by another's eyes.* Are these consequences really spelled out in the play? They are in the most specific fashion, in perfectly unambiguous statements that somehow never manage to be heard; and even when they are noticed, a label is immediately placed on them, canceling out their effectiveness. The following lines, for example, will be labeled "rhetorical," which means that they can be dismissed at will, treated as insignificant. Recall that when Helena seeks the secret of Hermia's power over Demetrius, Hermia answers:

> I frown upon him, yet he loves me still.
> HELENA: O that your frowns would teach my smiles such skill!
> HERMIA: I give him curses, yet he gives me love.
> HELENA: O that my prayers could such affection move!
> HERMIA: The more I hate, the more he follows me.
> HELENA: The more I love, the more he hateth me.
>
> (1.1.194–99)

It cannot be denied that there is a great deal of rhetoric in *A Midsummer Night's Dream.* Rhetoric in the pejorative sense means that certain figures of speech are repeated unthinkingly by people who do not even notice their meaning. The four protagonists of *A Midsummer Night's Dream* certainly are unthinking repeaters of modish formulas. But mere parodies of rhetorical vacuity would be themselves vacuous, and Shakespeare does not indulge in them. With him the most ex-hausted clichés can become bolts of lightning. When Helena calls Demetrius a "hard-hearted adamant," she speaks the most literal truth. Harshness and cruelty draw her and her friends as a magnet draws iron. The supposedly artificial figures of speech really describe the truth of desire with amazing exactitude. When an impeccably educated reader comes upon the lines, "Where is Lysander and fair Hermia? / The one I'll slay, the other slayeth me" (2.1.189–90), he feels a secret anxiety at the thought that a cultural monument like Shakespeare may be lapsing into less than impeccable taste. These lines are satirical; but, in order to be completely reassured, we have to know what the satirical intent is about. Shakespeare is not mocking a particular "rhet-oric" and a particular "bad taste." Considerations of "style" are mainly relevant to professors of literature. It is rather the whole language of passion, with its constant borrowings fro the fields of war, murder, and destruction, that Shakespeare is commenting upon. A book like De Rougemont's *Love in the Western World* throws more light on the type of meditation that nourishes Shakespearean satire than all stylistics put together. Shakespeare is almost contemporary in his recourse to the debased language of degraded human relations. With us, however, debased language generally remains just what it is and nothing more; the work never rises above the mire it pretends to stigmatize, or else it immediately sinks gently back into it. Not so with Shakespeare. The interest of the so-called rhetoric is its frightening pertinence; the destiny it spells for the four lovers, the destiny they unthinkingly announce, is really the one that they are busily forging for themselves; it is a tragic destiny from which they escape only by the sheer luck of being in a comedy.

This ambiguous nature of "rhetoric" is essential to the twofold nature of the play. As long as we listen as unthinkingly as the protagonists speak, we remain the superficial play which is made of "figures of speech," as well as of fairies and father figures. At the purely aesthetic and thematic level of "poetic imagination," we operate with the same conceptual tools as Theseus and the lovers; good and bad metaphors, true love turned false and false turned true. We understand little more than the lovers themselves. If, on the contrary, we stop long enough to hear what is being said, a pattern begins to emerge: the disquieting infrastructure of mimetic desire, which will erupt into hysterical violence a little later.

One of the most striking features in the amorous discourse of the protagonists is the abundance of animal images. These images express the self-abasement of the lover in front of his idol. As he vainly tries to reach for the absolute that appears incarnated in the model, the lover exalts his successful rival to greater and greater heights; as a result, he feels degraded to lower and lower depths. The first animal images appear immediately after Helena's hysterical celebration of her rival's beauty:

> No, no, I am as ugly as a bear.
> For beasts that meet me run away for fear
>
> . . . .
>
> What wicked and dissembling glass of mine
> Made me compare with Hermia's sphery eyne?
> (2.2.94–99)

We will be told once again that such images are "pure rhetoric"; their source has been identified: most of them, it appears, come from Ovid.

This is true, but the existence of a literary source for a figure of speech does not necessarily imply that it is used in a purely formal and inconsequential manner, that it cannot be given a vital significance by the second writer. It can be shown, I believe, that the animal images are part of the process which leads from mimetic desire to myth; this process is a continuous one, but a certain number of steps can be distiguished which have an existential as well as a functional significance. Far from raising himself to the state of a superman, a god, as he seeks to do, the subject of mimetic desire sinks to the level of animality. The animal images are the price the self has to pay for its idolatrous worship of otherness. This idolatry is really "selfish" in the sense that it is meant for the sake of the self; the self wants to appropriate the absolute that it perceives, but its extreme thirst for self-elevation results in extreme self-contempt, quite logically if paradoxically, since this self always meets and invites its own defeat at the hands of a successful rival.

Animal images are thus a direct consequence of the inordinate metaphysical ambition that makes desire mimetic. They are an integral part of the rigorous pattern I am trying to unravel; the law of that pattern could be defined by Pascal's aphorism, *Qui fait l'ange fait la bête.* The whole midsummer night looks like a dramatization of that aphorism. Here again is Helena, who *fait la bête* with Demetrius:

> I am your spaniel, and, Demetrius,
> The more you beat me, I will fawn on you.
> Use me but as your spaniel, spurn me, strike me,
> Neglect me, lose me—only give me leave,
> Unworthy as I am, to follow you.
> What worser place can I beg in your love—
> And yet a place of high respect with me—
> Than to be used as you use your dog?
>
> (2.1.203–10)

Partners in mimetic desire cannot think of each other as equal human beings; their relationship becomes less and less human; they are condemned to an angel-beast or superman-slave relationship. Helena's near worship of Hermia might be described, today, in terms of an "inferiority complex." But psychiatrists view their so-called complexes almost as physical entities, almost as independent and stable as the self they are supposed to affect. Shakespeare is alien to this substantial thinking; he sees everything in terms of relations. Helena's "inferiority complex," for example, is only the "wrong" or the "beast" end of her relationship with Hermia and Demetrius. Ultimately, everyone ends up with the same "inferiority complex," since everyone feels deprived of an absolute superiority that always appears to belong to someone else.

Being purely mimetic, this relationship is anchored in no stable reality; it is therefore bound to be unstable. The metaphysical absolute seems to shift from character to character. With each shift the entire configuration is reorganized, still on the basis of the same polarities, but reversed. The beast becomes a god and the god becomes a beast. Inferiority becomes superiority and vice versa. Up is down and down is up.

During the first scenes, Hermia, being worshiped by everyone, appears to be and feel divine. Helena, being truly rejected and despised, feels despicable. But then it is Helena's turn to be worshiped and Hermia feels like a despicable beast. After the initial moment of relative stability, the four lovers enter a world of more and more rapid reversals and inversions. The necessities of dramatic presentation force Shakespeare to be selective and somewhat schematic in his description of the process, but the principles at work are obvious. As soon as the midsummer night crisis begins in earnest, the animal metaphors are not only multiplied but turned upside down and jumbled together. As the reversals become more and more precipitous, we obviously move toward complete chaos. All this, of course, to the renewed chagrin of our guardians of "good taste," who do not see any purpose to this unseemly spectacle and view it as mere stylistic self-indulgence on the part of the author. The "rhetoric" was bad enough before, but now it is going out of its rhetorical mind. Here is Helena, once more, getting ready to chase Demetrius through the woods:

> Run when you will, the story shall be changed.
> Apollo flies, and Daphne holds the chase;
> The dove pursues the griffin; the mild hind
> Makes speed to catch the tiger.
>
> (2.1.230–33)

Reversal is so pervasive a theme in *A Midsummer Night's Dream,* as in most of Shakespeare's plays, that it finally extends to the whole of nature. Titania tells us, for example, that the seasons are out of turn. Scholars assume that the weather must have been particularly bad in the year Shakespeare wrote the play; this, in turn, gives some clues to the dating of the play. It must be true, indeed, that Shakespeare needed some really inclement weather to write what he did; however, the bad weather serves a specifically Shakespearean purpose, providing still another opportunity for more variations on the major theme of the play, the theme of differences reversed and inverted:

> The spring, the summer,
> The childing autumn, angry winter, change
> Their wonted liveries, and the mazed world,
> By their increase now knows not which is which.
>
> (2.1.111–14)

The very pervasiveness of reversal makes it impossible for commentators not to acknowledge the theme, but it also provides a means of minimizing its significance by shifting the emphasis where it should not be shifted, onto nature and the cosmos. This, of course, is exactly what myth itself does in its constant projection and expulsion of human violence. The nineteenth- and twentieth-century mythologists who asserted and still assert that myth is mostly a misreading of natural phenomena really perpetuate the mythical dissimulation and disguise of human violence. Shakespeare seems to be doing the same thing when he inserts his midsummer night into the poetic frame of a crisis of quasi-comic proportions. In that vast macrocosm, our four protagonists' antics appear as a tiny dot moved by forces beyond its own control, automatically relieved, once more, of all responsibility for whatever harm its even tinier components may be doing to one another and to themselves. Nature, in other words, must be included among the other mythical excuses, such as the mean father and the fairies. Shakespeare certainly gives it a major poetic and dramatic role, in keeping with the principles of what I earlier called the surface play. This is true; but, as in the other instances, he also makes sure that the truth becomes explicit. The real Shakespearean perspective is clearly suggested immediately below the lines just quoted. Titania ascribes disarray neither to herself nor to Oberon nor even to both, insofar as they would remain serene divinities manipulating humanity from outside, but to the *conflict* between them, a very human conflict, to be sure, which implies the same reversals of roles as the midsummer night and which duplicates perfectly the strife among the four lovers:

> And this same progeny of evils comes
> From our debate, from our dissensions;
> We are their parents and original.
>
> (2.1.115–17)

Reversals in nature are only reflections, metaphoric expressions, and poetic orchestrations of the mimetic crisis. Instead of viewing myth as a humanization of nature, as we always tend to do, Shakespeare views it as the naturalization as well as the supernaturalization of a very human violence. Specialists on the subject might be well advised to take a close look at this Shakespearean view; what if it turned out to be less mythical than their own!

The lopsided view that the lovers take of their own relationships keeps reversing itself with increasing speed. This constant exchange of the relative positions within the total picture is the cause of the vertigo, the loss of balance which the four characters experience. That feeling is inseparable from the sense of extreme difference to which the same characters never cease to cling, even as this difference keeps shifting around at a constantly accelerating tempo. It is in fact, to be sure, that two characters who face each other in fascination and rivalry can never occupy the same position together, since they themselves constitute the polarity that oscillates between them. They resemble a seesaw, with one rider always going up when the other is going down and vice versa. Never, therefore, do they cease to feel out of tune with each other, radically different from each other. In reality, of course, the positions successively occupied are the same; whatever difference remains is a purely *temporal* one which must become smaller and, as the movement keeps accelerating, even tend to zero, though without actually reaching it.

Even though they persevere in difference (an ever more vertiginous difference to be sure, but difference nevertheless), the protagonists become more and more undifferentiated. We have seen that the seasons lose their relative specificity, but the true loss of differentiation comes from the crisis among men who are caught in the vicious circle of mimetic desire. Progressive undifferentiation is not an illusion but the objective truth of the whole process, in the sense that reciprocity becomes more and more perfect. There is never anything on one side of a rivalry which, sooner or later, will not be found on the other. Here and there it is exactly the same mixture of fascination and hatred, the same curses, the same everything. It can be said that mimetic desire *really works*: it really achieves the goal it has set for itself, which is the *translation* of the follower into his model, the metamorphosis of one into the other, the absolute identity of all. As the climax of the midsummer night approaches, the four protagonists lose whatever individuality they formerly appeared to have; they wander like brutes in the forest, trading the same insults and finally the same physical blows, all drugged with the same drug, all bitten by the same serpent.

The more our characters tend to see one another in terms of black and white, the more alike they really *make* one another. Every slightest move, every single reaction becomes more and more immediately self-defeating. The more these characters deny the reciprocity among them, the more they bring it about, each denial being immediately reciprocated.

At the moment when difference should be most formidable, it begins to elude not one protagonist but the four of them all at once. Characters dissolve and personalities disintegrate. Glaring contradictions multiply, no firm judgment will hold. Each protagonist becomes a masked monster in the eyes of the other three, hiding his true being behind deceptive and shifting appearances. Each points at the hypocrite and the cheat in the others, partly in order not to feel that the ground is also slipping from under him. Helena, for example, accuses Hermia of being untrue to her real self: "Fie, fie! You counterfeit, you puppet, you!" (3.2.288). Hermia misunderstands and thinks Helena is making fun of her shortness:

> Puppet? Why so? Aye, that way goes the game.
> Now I perceive that she hath made compare
> Between our statures, she hath urged her height.
> And with her personage, her tall personage,
> Her height, forsooth, she hath prevailed with him.
> And are you grown so high in his esteem
> Because I am so dwarfish and so low?
> How low am I, thou painted maypole?
> How low am I? I am not yet so low
> But that my nails can reach unto thine eyes.
>
> (3.2.289–98)

C. L. Barber correctly observes that the four young people vainly try to interpret their conflicts through something "manageably related to their individual identities," but they never achieve their purpose:

> Only accidental differences can be exhibited. Helena tall, Hermia short. Although the men think that "reason says" now Helena is "the worthier maid," personalities have nothing to do with the case. . . . The life in the lovers' part is not to be caught in individual speeches, but by regarding the

> whole movement of the farce, which swings and spins each
> in turn through a common pattern, an evolution that seems
> to have an impersonal power of its own.

The time comes when the antagonists literally no longer know who they are: "Am I not Hermia? Are you not Lysander?" (3.2.273).

Here it is no exaggeration or undue modernization to speak of a "crisis of identity." To Shakespeare, however, the crisis is primarily one of differentiation. The four characters lose a self-identity which they and the philosophers would like to turn into an absolute and which becomes relative for that very reason; it is made to depend upon the otherness of a model. When Barber points out that Shakespeare fully intends for his characters, in the course of the play, to lose whatever distinctiveness they had or appeared to have at the beginning (which wasn't much anyway), he runs counter to a long tradition of criticism, the whole tradition of "realism" and of "psychology." Many critics do not find it conceivable that a writer like Shakespeare might be more interested in the undoing and dissolving of "characters" than in their creation, viewing as they do the latter task as the one assigned to all artists of all eternity. Only the most honest will face squarely their own malaise and formulate the obvious consequences of their own inadequate principles: they blame Shakespeare for "insufficient characterization."

The question is truly fundamental. The whole orientation of criticism depends on it. It is usually the wrong solution that is adopted, all the more blindly because it remains implicit. I personally believe that the conflictual undifferentiation of the four lovers is the basic Shakespearean relationship in both his tragedies and comedies. It is the relationship of the four *doubles* in *A Comedy of Errors*; it is the relationship of the Montagues and the Capulets, of course, but also of Caesar, Brutus, and his coconspirators, of Shylock and Bassanio, of all the great tragic and comic characters. There is no great theater without a gripping awareness that, far from sharpening our differences, as we like to believe, our violence obliterates them, dissolving them into that reciprocity of vengeance which becomes its own self-inflicted punishment. Shakespeare is fully aware, at the same time, that no theater audience can assume the full force of this revelation. Its impact must and will necessarily be blunted. Some violence will be made "good" and the rest "bad" at the expense of some sacrificial victim, with or without the complicity of the writer. There is no doubt that, in many instances, Shakespeare is a willing accomplice; but his is never an absolute betrayal of his own vision, because the differences he provides are always at the same time undermined and treated as quasi-allegories. An excessive appetite for "characterization" and catharsis will take nothing of this into account: it will systematically choose as most Shakespearean what really is least so, at least in the form in which it is chosen. It will thus provide not only our realistic stodginess but also our romantic self-righteousness with the only type of nourishment they can absorb.

It is in a comedy like *A Midsummer Night's Dream*, if we only agree to read through the transparence of the "airy nothing," that the truth will stare us most openly in the face. Far from lacking substance and profundity, as even George Orwell inexplicably maintained, this play provides a quintessence of the Shakespearean spirit.

Am I not "going too far" when I assimilate the midsummer night to the tragic crisis; am I not running the risk of betraying the real Shakespeare? The language of differences and undifferentiation is not Shakespeare's own, after all. This is true if we take the matter quite literally; but it is also true that Shakespeare, in some of his writing, comes close to using that same language. A case in point is the famous speech of Ulysses in *Troilus and Cressida:* it describes that very same crisis, but does so in purely theoretical language and on as vast a scale as the most ambitious tragedies, as the crisis of an entire culture. The speech is built around one single word, *degree,* which would certainly be condemned as too "abstract," too "philosophical," if it were applied to Shakespeare by anyone but Shakespeare himself. And obviously Shakespeare applies it to himself as well as to the Greeks: it is the social framework of tragedy which is at stake.

> O when degree is shaked,
> Which is the ladder to all high designs,
> The enterprise is sick! How could communities,
> Degrees in school, and brotherhoods in cities,
> Peaceful commerce from dividable shores,
> The primogenitive and due of birth,
> Prerogative of age, crowns, sceptres, laurels,
> But by degree, stand in authentic place?
> Take but degree away, untune that string,
> And, hark, what discord follows! Each thing meets
> In mere oppugnancy. The bounded waters

Should lift their bosoms higher than the shores,
And make a sop of all this solid globe;
Strength should be lord of imbecility,
And the rude son should strike his father dead;
Force should be right, or rather, right and wrong,
Between whose endless jar justice resides,
Should lose their names, and so should justice too.
Then every thing include itself in power,
Power into will, will into appetite;
And appetite, an universal wolf,
So doubly seconded with will and power,
Must make perforce an universal prey,
And last eat up himself.

(1.3.101–24)

The word *degree*, from the Latin *gradus* (step, degree, measure of distance), means exactly what is meant here by difference. Culture is conceived not as a mere collection of unrelated objects, but as a totality, or, if we prefer, a structure, a system of people and institutions always related to one another in such a way that a single differentiating principle is at work. This social transcendence does not exist as an object, of course. That is why, as soon as an individual member, overcome by *hubris,* tries to usurp Degree, he finds imitators; more and more people are affected by the contagion of mimetic rivalry, and Degree collapses, being nothing more than the mysterious absence of such rivalry in a functional society. The crisis is described as the "shaking," the "vizarding," or the taking away of Degree; all cultural specificities vanish, all identities disintegrate. Conflict is everywhere, and everywhere meaningless: *Each thing meets in mere oppugnancy.* We must note this use of the word "thing," the least determined, perhaps, in the English language. The meaningless conflict is that of the *doubles.* Unable to find a way out, men err and clash stupidly, full of hatred but deprived of real purpose; they resemble objects loose on the deck of a ship tossed about in a storm, destroying one another as they collide endlessly and mindlessly.

In the light of the above remarks, a precise analysis of the midsummer crisis becomes possible. The four protagonists do not see one another as *doubles*; they misunderstand their relationship as one of extreme if unstable differentiation. A point must finally be reached where all of these illusory differences oscillate so rapidly that the contrasting specificities they define are no longer perceived separately; they begin to impinge on one another, they appear to merge. Beyond a certain threshold, in other words, the dizziness mentioned earlier will make normal perception impossible; hallucination must prevail, of a type that can be ascertained with some precision, being not purely capricious and random but predetermined by the nature of the crisis.

When polarities such as the ones described earlier between the "beast" and the "angel" oscillate so fast that they become one, the elements involved remain too incompatible for a harmonious "synthesis," and they will simply be juxtaposed or superimposed on each other. A composite picture should emerge which will include fragments of the former "opposites" in a disorderly mosaic. Instead of a god and a beast facing each other as two independent and irreducible entities, we are going to have a mixture and a confusion of the two, a god that is a beast or a beast that is a god. When the polarities revolve fast enough, all antithetic images must be viewed simultaneously, through a kind of cinematic effect that will produce the illusion of a more or less single being in the form or rather the formlessness of "some monstrous shape."

What *A Midsummer Night's Dream* suggests, in other words, is that the mythical monster, as a conjunction of elements which normally specify different beings, automatically results from the more and more rapid turnover of animal and metaphysical images, a turnover which depends on the constantly self-reinforcing process of mimetic desire. We are not simply invited to witness the dramatic but insignificant birth of bizarre mythical creatures; rather we are confronted with a truly fascinating and important view of mythical genesis.

In a centaur, elements specific to man and to horse are inexplicably conjoined, just as elements specific to man and ass are conjoined in the monstrous metamorphosis of Bottom. Since there is no limit to the differences that can be jumbled together, since the picture will necessarily remain blurred, the diversity of monsters will appear properly limitless and the infinite seems to be at hand. Insofar as separate entities can be distinguished within the monstrous whole, there will be individual monsters; but they will have no stability: they will constantly appear to merge and marry one another. The birth of monsters, their scandalous commingling with human beings, and the wedding of the one with the other, all these mythical phenomena are part of one and the same experience. The wedding of Titania with the ass-headed Bottom, under the influence of that same "love juice" that makes the lovers crazy, can take place only because the difference between the natural and the supernatural is gone; haughty Titania finds to her dismay that the barrier between her and ordinary mortals is down:

> Tell me how it came this night
> That I sleeping there was found
> With these mortals on the ground.
>
> (4.1.103–5)

The conjunction of man, god, and beast takes place at the climax of the crisis and is the result of a process which began with the play itself. It is the ultimate metamorphosis, the supreme *translation*.

In that process the animal images play a pivotal role. I noted earlier that their perfect integration into the disquieting symphony conducted by Shakespeare was not at all incompatible with their identification as literary reminiscences. We must now go further. To say that these images are compatible with the role that Shakespeare himself wants them to play in his own work is no longer enough. It is evident that these animal images are especially appropriate to that role and that Shakespeare has selected them for that reason. Most of them come from Ovid's *Metamorphoses*. They are directly implicated in an earlier genesis of myth, still quite mythical, and far removed from the obviously psychosocial interpretation implicitly proposed by Shakespeare. It is no exaggeration to assert that *A Midsummer Night's Dream*, because it is a powerful reinterpretation of Ovid, also provides, at least in outline, Shakespeare's own genetic theory of myth. It is a mistake, therefore, to view the animal images as if they were suspended in midair between the matter-of-fact interplay of desires on the one hand and purely fantastic shapes on the other. They are the connecting link between the two. Thus we can no longer see the play as a collage of heterogeneous elements, as another monstrosity; it is a continuous development, a series of logically related steps that will account even for the monsters in its own midst if they are only followed to the end, if enough trust is placed in the consistency of the author.

At the climax of the crisis, Demetrius and Lysander are about to kill each other, but Puck, on Oberon's orders, substitutes himself for the *doubles* and puts the four lovers to sleep. When they wake up the next morning, they find themselves reconciled, neatly arranged this time in well-assorted couples. Good weather is back, everything is in order once more. Degree is restored. Theseus appears upon the scene. He and his future wife hear an account of the midsummer night, and it is for the duke to pronounce the final word, to draw the official conclusion of the whole episode in response to a slightly anxious question asked by Hippolyta. Then comes the most famous passage of the entire play. Theseus dismisses the entire midsummer night as the inconsequential fruit of a gratuitous and disembodied imagination. He seems to believe that the real question is whether or not to believe in the fairies. Hippolyta's later words will reveal that her concern is of an entirely different sort; but, like all rationalists of a certain type, Theseus has a marvelous capacity for simplifying the issues and displacing a debate toward his favorite stomping ground. Much of what he says is true, of course; but it is beside the point. To believe or not to believe, that is *not* the question; and, by trumpeting his fatuous skepticism, Theseus dispenses himself from looking at the remarkable pattern of the midsummer night and the disturbing clues it may contain concerning the nature of all social beliefs, including his own. Who knows if the crisis and its cathartic resolution are responsible only for the monsters of the night? Who knows if the peace and order of the morning after, if even the majestic confidence of the unchallenged ruler are not equally in their debt? Theseus' casual dismissal of myth is itself mythical in the sense that it will not ask such questions. There is irony in the choice of a great mythical figure to embody this rationalistic dismissal. Here Theseus acts as the high priest of a benign casting-out of all disturbing phenomena under the triple heading of poetry, lunacy, and love. This neat operation frees respectable men of all responsibility for whatever tricks, past, present, and future, their own desires and mimetic violence might play on them, thus perfectly duplicating the primary genesis of myth, the one that I have just noted.

> HIPPOLYTA: 'Tis strange, my Theseus, that these lovers
>   speak of.
> THESEUS: More strange than true. I never may believe
>   These antique fables, nor these fairy toys.
>   Lovers and madmen have such seething brains,
>   Such shaping fantasies, that apprehend
>   More than cool reason ever comprehend.
>   The lunatic, the lover, and the poet
>   Are of imagination all compact.
>   One sees more devils than vast Hell can hold,
>   That is the madman. The lover, all as frantic,
>   Sees Helen's beauty in a brow of Egypt.

> The poet's eye, in a fine frenzy rolling,
> Doth glance from heaven to earth, from earth to heaven,
> And as imagination bodies forth
> The form of things unknown, the poet's pen
> Turns them to shapes, and gives to airy nothings
> A local habitation and a name.
> Such tricks hath strong imagination
> That if it would but apprehend some joy,
> It comprehends some bringer of that joy;
> Or in the night, imagining some fear,
> How easy is a bush supposed a bear!
>
> (5.1.1–22)

This positivism *avant la lettre* seems to contradict much of what I have said so far. Evidence so laboriously assembled seems scattered once more. Where are the half-concealed yet blatant disclosures, the allusive ambiguities artfully disposed by the author (or so I supposed) for our enlightenment? Long before I came to it, I am sure, many skeptical readers had the passage in mind, and they will rightly want to know how it fits into my reading. Here it is, finally, an obvious ally of the traditional readings that quite naturally regard it as the unshakable rock upon which they are founded. As such, it must constitute a formidable stumbling block for my own intricate revisionism.

The lead is provided by Shakespeare himelf, and the present status of the passage as a piece of anthology, a *lieu commun* of modern aestheticism, testifies to the willingness of posterity to take up that lead. The reading provided by Theseus is certainly the most pleasant, the one which conforms to the wishes of the heart and to the tendency of the human mind not to be disturbed. We must note, besides, that the text is centrally located, placed in the mouth of the most distinguished character, couched in sonorous and memorable phrases, well fit to adorn academic dissertations on the so-called "imaginative faculty."

This speech has been so successful, indeed, that no one ever pays any attention to the five quiet lines that follow. Hippolyta's response does not have the same resounding eloquence, but the dissatisfaction she expresses with the slightly pompous and irrelevant *postmortem* of Theseus *was written by Shakespeare himself.* It cannot fail to be of immense significance:

> But the story of the night told over,
> And all their minds transfigured so together,

More witnesseth than fancy's images,
And grows to something of great constancy,
But howsoever strange and admirable.

(5.1.23–27)

Hippolyta clearly perceives Theseus' failure to come up with the holistic interpretation that is necessary. He and his innumerable followers deal with the play as if it were a collection of separate cock-and-bull stories. To them imagination is a purely individual activity, unrelated to the interplay of the four lovers. They themselves are the true inheritors of myth when they confidently believe in their simplistic objectivity. They see myth as something they have already left behind with the greatest of ease, as an object of passing amusement, perhaps, when the occasion arises to watch some light entertainment such as *A Midsummer Night's Dream*.

There is no doubt that we are dealing with two critical attitudes and that Shakespeare himself vindicates the one that has always been least popular. When I suggest that *A Midsummer Night's Dream*, behind all the frills, is a serious genetic theory of myth, I am only translating the five lines of Hippolyta into contemporary parlance. It is not I but Shakespeare who writes that the midsummer night is more than a few graceful arabesques about English folklore and Elizabethan lovers. It is not I but Shakespeare who draws our attention to *all their minds transfigured so together* and to the final result as *something of great constancy*, in other words, a common structure of mythical meaning.

I have suggested that *A Midsummer Night's Dream* might well be two plays in one. This hypothesis is now strengthened. At this point, the two plays are coming to life as individuals; they are speaking to us and to each other, one through Theseus, the other through Hippolyta. The exchange between the bridegroom and his acutely perceptive but eternally overshadowed bride amounts to the first critical discussion of the play. Representing as he does blissful ignorance and the decorum of Degree enthroned, Theseus must hold the stage longer, speaking with a brilliance and finality that confirms the dramatic preeminence of the surface play, a preeminence that is maintained throughout. Since he gives a voice to all these—the immense majority—who want nothing more in such an affair than "airy nothings," Theseus must be as deaf and blind to his bride's arguments as Shakespeare's audiences and critics seem to have been ever since. The debate seems onesided in the duke's favor, but how could we fail, at this juncture, to realize that the real last word belongs to Hippolyta, both literally and figuratively?

In the context of the evidence gathered earlier, how could we doubt that Hippolyta's words are the decisive ones, that they represent Shakespeare's own view of how the play really hangs together? If we really understand that context, we cannot be surprised that Shakespeare makes his correction of Theseus as discreet and unobstrusive as it is illuminating, visible only to the same thoughtful attention already needed to appreciate such pregnant ambiguities as "to choose love by another's eyes" and other similar gems of exquisitely direct, yet almost imperceptible revelation.

Hippolyta is gently tugging at Theseus' sleeve, but Theseus hears nothing. Posterity hears nothing. Hippolyta has been tugging at that sleeve for close to four hundred years now, with no consequence whatever, her words forever buried under the impressive scaffoldings of Degree once more triumphant in the guise of rationalism, eternally silenced by that need for reassurance which is answered first by belief in myths, then by a certain kind of disbelief. Shakespeare seems to give his blessing to both, ironically confounded in the person of Theseus. He places in the hands of his pious and admiring betrayers the instruments best designed to blunt the otherwise intolerably sharp edge of their favorite bard's genius.

"A Little O'erparted": Actors and Audiences in *A Midsummer Night's Dream*

Alvin B. Kernan

The theater is a public art and the playwright therefore works under vastly different conditions than the poet. What the playwright has to say must be said through the voices and styles of the actors, and it must be played on a particular stage in a particular theatrical building, all of which affects the playwright's original intentions. The play's ultimate statement will in large part be what those who produce it make of it, and its meaning will finally be determined by the response of an audience made up of many different people of widely varying interests and capabilities. When the performance ends the play disappears as if it had never been, and if it is played again it will take a new form from adjustments made in the playhouse, from the presence of new actors, and from the inevitable changes in the tone and style of performance from day to day. No play is ever the same play twice running. Even if the play is eventually fixed in print it is always, even under the best of circumstances, difficult to establish the text which represents the "true" play, and any printed text will always be only the bare bones of something that was designed for the stage and can achieve its full reality only in the transitory color, light, voices, and movements of the theater. Furthermore, because the production of a play involves large numbers of people and the use of expensive materials and property, the theater inevitably becomes entangled in complex economic issues. Being a public affair, openly staged out in the world

From *The Playwright as Magician: Shakespeare's Image of the Poet in the English Public Theatre.* © 1979 by Yale University. Yale University Press, 1979.

before the eyes of large numbers of its citizens, a play also affects society and must face the question of its relationship to the state and its governors, who inevitably try to use and control such a powerful means of propaganda.

All these conditions of theater work together to diminish the importance of the playwright's role in the creation of art and to place into question the existence of the work of art in any absolute, ideal sense. It is difficult for a playwright to conceive of himself as a heroic poet like Petrarch or a courtly poet like Sidney, and equally difficult for him to think of his play as a perfect artifact, wrought from his own vision and standing forever as an unchanging image of truth and beauty. A courtly sonneteer like Shakespeare's Poet might boast that "Not marble, nor the gilded monuments / Of princes, shall outlive this powr'ful rhyme," but a writer for the theater knows that no man and no playwright

> is the lord of anything—
> Though in and of him there be much consisting—
> Till he communicate his parts to others.
> Nor doth of himself know them for aught
> Till he behold them formed in th' applause
> Where they're extended
>
> (*Troilus*, 3.3.115–20)

The very nature of theater as a public art forces these realizations on any playwright at any time, but the actual conditions in which Elizabethan plays were written and produced intensified the playwrights' awareness that a poet and his plays were only a part of a much larger grouping of people, traditions, and social forces interacting in complex ways to produce theater. A poet like Petrarch or Sidney could, because of his favored social position and freedom from economic pressures, see poetry as high art, ideal truth, and the expression of personal genius. An Elizabethan playwright working for money in the public theater, having to consider the interests of his audience and the nature of his playing company and physical theater, could be far less certain that his work was art, that it expressed his own genius, or that its value extended beyond today's performance.

The sons for the most part of lower-class artisans and middle-class tradesmen—scriveners, bricklayers, cobblers, glovemakers—in many cases the first in their families to have received even a grammar school education, the Elizabethan playwrights were the first of that long line of poor but gifted writers—Johnson and Garrick, Gogol, Balzac—who made the mythic journey from the country to the capital city to earn fame and fortune by their art. Patronage did not really function for them, the book trade could not yet adequately support them, and so the surplus of talented young men whose humanist literary educations made the profession of writing seem both important and feasible found employment in the only place they could, the new theatrical repertory companies with their need for hundreds of plays a year.

Robert Greene's *Groatsworth of Wit Bought with a Million of Repentance,* in which he attacks Shapespeare as a mere actor who has begun to "bombast out a blank verse" in competition with his betters, and the academic *Parnassus Plays* written at Cambridge, tell of the indignation that educated authors felt at their treatment in the theater, where most either sank without a trace or became hacks turning out plays as commodities. Only a few really became successful playwrights. We know the titles of over a thousand plays written by identifiable authors between 1590 and 1642, and of these nearly half were written by a group of only twenty-two men who became the real professionals of the theater. Thomas Heywood, the most prolific of this group, wrote or had a hand in two hundred and twenty, but Shakespeare, who wrote thirty-eight, or a little less than two a year during his working life, is more characteristic of the hard-working professional.

The playwrights, at least the better ones, never surrendered their status as poets nor conceded that their plays were less than art, but their plays reveal not certainty but a deep unresolved tension between conceptions of the theater as an unlimited artistic power and as mere clownish spectacle. The magic which Marlowe's great philosopher Doctor Faustus commands is an idealized form of the playwright's ability to transform the world on his stage into the images of desire, producing grapes in winter or bringing Helen of Troy to life. But Faustus sells his soul for this absolute theatrical power, and even he finds in the end that he can create only transitory and unsatisfactory images. The clock strikes twelve as he disappears into Hell to pay with his soul for what have come to seem to him trivial powers, and the epigraph "Terminat hora diem, Terminat author opus" drives home the identification of damned magician with disenchanted playwright. Artistic anxiety is even more openly expressed by Jonson's *Volpone,* where the enormous energy and power of playing appear in perverse form as the rich merchant Volpone, the "great imposter," who acts out a pretense of sickness on the curtained stage of his great bed in order to satisfy his lust, his greed, and his desire for power. The Protean ability of Shakespeare's Richard III to change shapes at will, like the actor to whom he is frequently compared, frees him from limits imposed by his twisted body and a desperate time, but he uses his theatrical powers to deceive, to kill, and to attack society.

The theatrical self-consciousness of the Elizabethan and Jacobean dramatists has been much commented upon, and there has recently been a growing reaction against the view that the dramatists, particularly Shakespeare, were so obsessed with critical questions and aesthetics that, whatever the ostensible subject of their plays, all are ultimately "metadrama"—all plays, that is, about the nature of playing. I would agree that the artist's preoccupation with theory and his own role as a poet is predominantly a romantic and postromantic development resulting from the increasingly problematic nature of art in a scientific, utilitarian world. But the evidence is undeniable that the English Renaissance dramatists did concern themselves in their plays in obvious ways with the function of art and the proper nature of playing. They did so, however, at least in the first instance, not because of some deep philosophical commitment to theoretical issues, but out of a need to resolve the very real tensions created by a situation in which the writers' conception of the nature and value of their art did not square with the actual circumstances in which their plays were written and produced, or with the popular valuation of their work.

The English drama of the Renaissance has for so long been thought of in Romantic terms as the highest of the high arts, the glory of Literature, that it is now difficult to understand in what low esteem plays and stage were held during the great dramatic period in England from the building of the first professional playhouse in London in 1576 to the closing of the theaters by the Puritans in 1642. It was not that drama itself was despised, for the Roman dramatists, and to a lesser degree the Greeks, were studied, admired, translated, imitated, and performed in aristocratic and academic settings. Drama was widely understood, except by the more radical Puritans, who abominated all playing as pagan pretense and idleness, to be a high art with a long tradition of greatness in presenting moral truths and advising princes in memorable and powerful ways.

The theater that was despised, feared, and mocked was a professional theater which evolved during the sixteenth century from mummings and agricultural festivals, the old biblical cycles and public pageants, juggling acts and morality plays, morris dances and courtly entertainments. Professional acting companies formed during the fifteenth century and toured the country, playing on trestle stages in inn yards and public squares, before the screen in great halls of noble houses and guildhalls, in churches and in chapter houses. We have a vivid portrait of such a company in John Marston's play, *Histriomastix,* written about 1599, satirical in intent but furnishing some idea of what touring companies in earlier and later times probably were like. Several idle artisans, Gulch, Clout, Belch, Gut, and Incle, combine to form a playing company. They hire as their playwright the hack poet, Master Posthaste, call in a scrivener to draw up articles, choose the name of "Sir Oliver Owlet's Men" and the badge of "an owl in an ivy bush" for their company. They assemble a repertory of plays to fit every type of audience and set off with a wardrobe of new costumes, obtained on credit, to tour the countryside, singing their song:

> Some up and some downe, ther's Players in the towne,
> > You wot well who they bee:
> The summe doth arise, to three companies,
> > One, two, three, foure, make wee.
> Besides we that travell, with pumps full of gravell,
> > Made all of such running leather:
> That once in a weeke, new maisters wee seeke,
> > And never can hold together.

When Sir Oliver's Men reach a town they send out one of their players to the square, where he mounts the steps of the market-cross and cries out a play to be given in the town hall at three o'clock in the afternoon. Soon afterwards they are invited to play in the hall of a local noble where, after putting on a grotesque morality play, *The Prodigall Child,* they are paid three shillings and four pence. Inept as they are, they prosper and become proud, until they fall athwart the law and all of them are pressed into service and shipped overseas to fight in foreign wars.

With the construction in 1576, just to the north of the London wall, of the first of many permanent playhouses, the public theater began to stabilize in London—though the companies were still forced frequently to tour—with daily performances, distinguished star actors, professional playwrights, and a more solid financial base. As Christopher Hill makes clear, this new professional theater, however closely it may have been related to older theatrical traditions, constituted a revolutionary change in the conditions in which art was produced:

> The way in which capitalist relations came to pervade all sectors of society can be illustrated from an industry not often considered by economic historians—the entertainments industry. Before 1577 theatrical productions had been small-scale, once a week at most, either private performances by the dependants of a great lord or the amateur productions of a community, whether guild, Oxford or Cambridge college, or one of the Inns of Court. The financial genius of James Burbage brought playing from a small-scale private enterprise to a big business. The Theatre and the Curtain were both opened during 1577 [sic] with the object of producing plays to which the general public would be admitted on payment. The capital for the Globe was provided in part by the actors themselves, on a joint-stock basis. For prudential reasons the patronage of the royal family or of leading aristocrats was retained (under an Act of 1572 actors not so protected could be treated as vagabonds), but henceforth the profit motive prevailed. The drama was the first of the arts to be put on sale to the general public. Larger theatres brought bigger profits if the dramatist could draw his public. This created exciting new possibilities for writers, though capitalism had its drawbacks too. "Should these fellows come out of my debt," said the biggest theatre-financer of all, Philip Henslowe, under James I, "I should have no rule with them." It was this quite new commercialism in the theatre, plus the fact that the new theatrical buildings were outside the City and so immune from control by the City authorities, that led to the so-called "Puritan" attack on the stage—which in origin was not Puritan at all and was restricted to an attack on the commercial stage.
>
> (*Reformation to Industrial Revolution,* vol. 2, 1530–1780, of The Pelican Economic History of Britain)

Like all popular theater, this was primarily an actor's theater, and the actors organized themselves in the manner common in other business enterprises of the day, as a guild or company of master craftsmen, setting standards of workmanship, limiting membership, and training their successors. But as Hill reminds us, "We should certainly not be sentimental about guilds in our period, whatever they may or may not have been earlier. They were usually controlled by oligarchies, and were often employers' rings." In the tradition of the craft guild system, each of the principal actors had his apprentice, bound to him for the usual period of seven years, during which time he was provided for by the master craftsman and taught his trade. These apprentices supplied the company with the necessary extra actors, and also, with their high voices and beardless faces, played the female roles. If times were prosperous, the numbers of the company would be swelled by hired actors who worked for a straight wage, and by the necessary technicians: bookkeepers, musicians, gatekeepers, sound-effect men and the like. A well-to-do company installed in a London theater might employ as many as between sixty and eighty men, where the earlier traveling groups consisted of only four to six players.

The presence in an acting company of eight or ten permanent players, who as "sharers" had controlling financial interest in the company, tended to set the acting techniques and styles of the company. These were repertory companies in the true sense, and each of the players had a standard type part and a personal acting style. In the Lord Chamberlain's Men, after 1603 the King's Men, William Shakespeare's company, the major actor was Richard Burbage who played the leading parts—Hamlet, Lear, Antony, Othello—from his first known appearance in the theater around 1590 to his death in 1619. The clown of the company was originally Will Kemp, the most famous comedian of his day. Jigs and other dances were his trademark, and at one time he jigged all the way from London to Norwich. Encouraged by this success, he set out to dance his way over the Alps to Italy, but gave up the attempt, though he did go on to Italy and played for a time in the *Commedia dell' Arte* there, and his easy transition to this extempory theater suggests that there must have been a good deal of stock farce and improvisation in the English public theater. Shakespeare was himself an actor in his company, as well as resident playwright, but of his acting line we know little, though tradition has it that he played older parts such as the Ghost in *Hamlet*.

When an Elizabethan dramatist wrote a play he had to keep in mind the abilities and preferences of such actors and the acting capabilities of the particular company. If the company did not have a boy capable of playing female parts really well, then it would be folly to write plays such as *Romeo and Juliet*, *Antony and Cleopatra*, or *The Winter's Tale*, all plays in which there are leading female roles. As long as Kemp was the company clown, the fools in the plays performed by his company were of the buffoonish, slapstick type—Gobbo or Dogberry. After Kemp left the company and Robert Armin began playing the clown's part, the fools became more subtle, ironic, and melancholy— the Fool in [*King*] *Lear*, and Feste in *Twelfth Night*.

But the actors controlled the plays they played in in even more direct ways. Shakespeare enjoyed a favored relationship with the King's Men as an actor, a sharer, resident playwright, and part owner of the Globe and Blackfriars theaters in which his company played. But something like the more usual way in which plays were written is suggested by the manner in which Philip Henslowe, a builder of theaters and an early entertainment entrepreneur, and his son-in-law, Edward Alleyn, the leading tragedian of the Admiral's Men, contracted for their plays from such freelance writers as Henry Chettle, Thomas Heywood, Anthony Munday, and Thomas Dekker. Henslowe, whose income depended partly on the gate at his theater, would pay a playwright a fee ranging from a few shillings to two pounds for a rough outline of a plot which had theatrical possibilities. The actors would then look at the outline and suggest changes. Then Henslowe would hire from one to as many as five playwrights to go to work on the play, presumably assigning each to work on his specialty, though he at times seems to have simply given each an act to write.

At this stage in the proceedings, Henslowe would advance to his author or authors a certain amount of money, perhaps as much as a pound, and when the play was completed and accepted, he would pay the rest of the money due, if the needy playwrights had not, as was often the case, obtained advances to live on in the meantime. With the finished play in hand, the actors would again go over it, and if there were parts they did not like, or which they thought could be bettered, Henslowe might pay perhaps ten shillings to one of the original authors for additions and changes, or he might call in a new specialist to write some more dialogue or add a spectacular scene. Not only were new plays constructed in this manner, but old favorites owned by the company were frequently refurbished in similar ways to bring them up to date.

The control of the actors over their plays were ultimately almost absolute. The acting company commissioned the plays, paying on the average about six pounds in the 1590s, which, as Gerald Bentley points out, was a fairly good wage when ten pounds was a schoolmaster's annual wage and forty shillings the usual payment by a printer for a book. Later the rate rose to as high as twenty pounds, but even in the 1590s a busy playwright could make twenty to thirty pounds a year. In return for these payments, however, the delivered play became the absolute property of the players, and they could and did change the play in any way they wished. Radical changes were likely in a popular play which remained in repertory for several years, and these changes often were made by a resident play-fixer, an actor beefing up a part, or by some outside writer, not necessarily the original author. As a result of all this changing in the theater, the text of a play was never really fixed, and many plays have consequently come down to us in such radically different versions that it becomes genuinely questionable whether we can say that a play ever had an absolute form or we can establish a "true text." Furthermore, it seems not to have been in the interest of the players to print the successful plays in their repertory lest their availability for reading reduce attendance at the theater; and so the plays were guarded rather carefully and often found their way to the printer only when the texts were pirated, usually in a corrupted form, or when some disaster such as the breakup of a company or the prohibition of playing because of plague forced a company to sell off its assets.

Dramatists thus found themselves in a new economic and artistic status as writers for wages, or as entrepreneurs who produced goods for the entertainment marketplace and depended for a living on the saleability of their commodity. It was difficult to think of what they produced under these circumstances as art expressing a poet's genius and winning him eternal fame by its perfect and permanent form. Instead, the actual facts of production defined plays as an amusement product, written on commission, often put together in collaboration, shaped to the styles and interests of particular actors, constantly changing form in the theater, used up in production, and dependent on pleasing for a moment the tastes of "Dukes and ambassadors, gentlemen and captains, citizens and apprentices, ruffians and harlots, 'Tailers, Tinkers, Cordwayners, Saylers, olde Men, yong Men, Women, Boyes, Girles, and such like.' (Stephen Gosson, *Playes Confuted in Five Actions*)."

It was this audience on which the income of the theaters and of the playwrights depended, and no poets had previously faced and had to please a large public of this particular kind and with this degree of power over art. The courtly poet had purposely limited his audience to a small, select group, and the new professional poets of the latter sixteenth century, like Spenser or Donne, had also addressed only a patron and a small circle of men with similar aristocratic tastes. But the English playwrights now found themselves paid and judged by a group very different from the small intellectual and social world which had previously been the audience for art.

The Elizabethan theater audience was a large one. Alfred Harbage in his authoritative study, *Shakespeare's Audience,* concludes that the capacity of the Elizabethan public theaters was between 2,500 and 3,000, and that the average daily attendance in 1595 at one London theater, the Rose, was slightly over 1,000. Greater London then had a population of about 160,000, and Harbage estimates that 21,000, or about 13 percent, went to the theater in any given performance week in 1605. The audience seems to have been as various as it was large, but on the exact nature of that variety the evidence and the conclusions which scholars have drawn from it are contradictory. Most of the contemporary descriptions of the audience are written from a hostile, often a Puritan, point of view and portray the "common haunters" of the theater as

> the leaudest persons in the land, apt for pilferie, periurie, forgerie, or any rogories, the very scum, rascallitie, and baggage of the people, thieues, cut-purses, shifters, cousoners; briefly an vncleane generation, and spaune of vipers: must not here be good rule, where is such a broode of Hell-bred creatures? for a Play is like a sincke in a Towne, wherevnto all the filth doth runne: or the byle in the body, that draweth all the ill humours vnto it.
>
> (HENRY CROSSE, *Vertues Commonwealth* [1603])

Attacks such as this provided the basis for the long-accepted view of Shakespeare's audience as idle apprentices, thieves, whores, young gallants, and a group of people who in general would presumably not have been much interested in art. But in his thorough and convincing survey of the evidence, Alfred Harbage rejects this older view and finds instead "a large and receptive assemblage of men and women of all ages and all classes," predominantly working class, decent, cheerful, quiet, and capable of understanding in large measure the plays they saw.

> I should guess that the audience as a whole understood and appreciated what it bought and approved. Its approval could

not have been easy to win. . . . Shakespeare's audience was literally popular, ascending through each gradation from potboy to prince. It was the one to which he had been conditioned early and for which he had never ceased to write. It thrived for a time, it passed quickly, and its like has never existed since. It must be given much of the credit for the greatness of Shakespeare's plays.

Whatever the exact nature of the audience may have been—and the evidence suggests that it was far more likely to have been a cross-section of London, with a predominance of educated and intelligent people than "a broode of Hellbred creatures"—there is no question that Shakespeare pleased it with plays that only rarely pandered to low or debased tastes. We know this not only from the fact that he prospered and became a rich man from his involvement with the theater, but also from the contemporary tributes paid him as the greatest and most popular of the English playwrights. A real sense of his popularity and the excitement that the plays created in the theater can be felt in the lines Leonard Digges wrote for inclusion in the 1640 edition of Shakespeare's poems:

> So have I seene, when Cesar would appeare,
> And on the Stage at half-sword parley were,
> *Brutus* and *Cassius*: oh how the Audience
> Were ravish'd, with what wonder they went thence,
>
> . . . .
> let but *Falstaffe* come,
> *Hall, Poines,* the rest you scarce shall have a roome
> All is so pester'd: let but *Beatrice*
> And *Benedicke* be seene, loe in a trice
> The Cockpit Galleries, Boxes, all are full
> To heare *Maluoglio* that crosse garter'd Gull.

Shakespeare was remarkable among the playwrights of the time for the close relationship he maintained with his fellow actors in the company which produced his plays, and for the popularity he enjoyed with his large audience from early on in his career. But his success in dealing with these two new and crucial factors in the creation of art did not apparently make him any the less wary of them or the less concerned about the part they had to play in the theater if his plays were to achieve the effects he conceived as being within the possibility of great dramatic art. References in his plays to actors and to acting are on balance negative, and the audiences he portrays on stage are never ideal but always something less than satisfactory in their behavior and their comprehension. Of all the English dramatists, Shakespeare seems to have been torn most severely between the conception of his plays as high art and as mere entertainment, and Philip Edwards rightly calls him "the experimenter, engaged in a continuous battle, a quarter of a century long, against his own skepticism about the value of his art as a model of human experience." He left us no direct critical statements about the issue, of course, but instead explored the question in his plays by allowing his characters and his scenes to state and to pose again and again the fundamental theatrical problems. His concerns and his developing understanding of the theater are imaged most sharply and summarily in the little internal plays, the plays-within-the-play, which, as Leslie Fiedler puts it, allow a play to provide "a history of itself, a record of the scruples and the hesitations of its maker in the course of its making, sometimes even a defense or definition of the kind to which it belongs or the conventions which it respects." ("The Defense of the Illusion and the Creation of Myth, Device and Symbol in the Plays of Shakespeare," in *English Institute Essays, 1948*, ed. D.A. Robertson, Jr.). Shakespeare's scruples and hesitations about the effect of actors and audiences on his plays are focused in three of his early plays, *The Taming of the Shrew, Love's Labour's Lost,* and *A Midsummer Night's Dream*, where internal plays are staged in such a way as to reveal the nature of the doubts a practicing playwright had about the ability of actors to present, and audiences to understand and be properly moved by, the poet's "most rare vision."

But it is always well to remember that Shakespeare is the most elusive of writers, the most difficult to find in his plays. The nature of the theatrical medium and his own ways of thinking and working combined to create plays which do not show us clear, direct statements of set moral or intellectual attitudes, but rather offer us the mystery of human motivation concealed behind words and actions, and a multiplicity of points of view and ambiguous events which encourages a variety of interpretations and meanings. If we are to find in his plays what Shakespeare himself thought about the theater, it must be by an elaborate process of triangulation, or by trying to catch a fleeting reflection in an extended series of mirrors. . . .

In his first decade as a dramatist, Shakespeare seems to have been on the whole optimistic about the power of playing to affect, even in less than ideal circumstances, the real world. He laughs at actors for their clumsiness and audiences for their literal-mindedness, chiding both for their inability to forget themselves and enter fully into the play; but the laughter, while it bears witness to some uneasiness on the part of the dramatist about his theater, seems in many ways merely the graceful modesty of an accomplished and self-assured professional dramatic poet continuing the proud humanistic tradition of claiming high value for his theatrical art. Nowhere is the modesty so complete, and at the same time the claim for the potential value of playing so extensive, as in *A Midsummer Night's Dream,* where Shakespeare dramatizes Sidney's boast that in place of nature's brazen world the poet creates a golden one, that imagination can perceive and art reveal an unseen reality just beyond the range of the senses and of the rational mind. In the *Dream,* art is no longer defined only by its ability to shape and transform an obstinate reality, as in [*The Taming of the*] *Shrew* and *Love's Labour's Lost,* but is shown to have an ability to penetrate the screen of the immediate world and reveal an imaginative truth that lies behind it.

Again Shakespeare glances, with an amusement that still betrays uneasiness, at the crudities of actors and stage and at the limitations of audiences. No players could be more hopeless than Nick Bottom the weaver and his mechanical friends who, in the hope of winning a small pension, perform the internal play, *Pyramus and Thisbe,* to celebrate the marriage of Duke Theseus of Athens to the Amazon queen, Hippolyta. Bottom's company, a parody of the amateur players and provincial touring companies who performed in aristocratic houses on special occasions, is so literal-minded as to require that the moon actually shine on the stage, that the wall through which Pyramus and Thisbe speak be solidly there, and that the actor who plays the lion assure the ladies in the audience, lest they be afraid, that he is only a make-believe lion. The deficiency of imagination which lies behind such a laughable conception of theater, carries over into the playing style of the actors as well. Their stumbling rant, missed cues, mispronounced words and lines, willingness to converse directly with the audience, doggerel verse, and general ineptitude, constitute a playwright's nightmare and completely destroy any possibility of creating the necessary illusion. As one critic describes it:

actors do intervene between audience and playwright. The play clearly indicates that intervention, and, as Bottom demonstrates in his failure as an actor, the actor, like the playwright, must be able both to perceive and to express the imaginative idea if the play is to be successful. For Bottom's audience to imagine a credible Pyramus, Bottom the actor's Pyramus, as well as Bottom the playwright's Pyramus, must be credible. If the playlet is to succeed, both the playwright's and actor's Pyramuses must be believably dead. Long before Bottom rises with his assurances that he is alive, the imaginative expression has been so disrupted that the audience's imaginative perception is prevented. Imagination cannot amend the matter; judgment takes over, and judgment tells us that this is the silliest matter that we have ever heard.

(RICHARD HENZE, *"A Midsummer Night's Dream*: Analogous Image")

The audience at *Pyramus and Thisbe*, Duke Theseus, his queen Hippolyta, and the young lovers who attend them, are socially superior to the actors but little more sophisticated about their proper roles in making a play work. Theseus does understand that, though this may be "the silliest stuff" ever heard, it lies within the power of a gracious audience to improve it, for "The best in this kind are but shadows; and the worst are no worse, if imagination amend them" (5.1.211–12). But the noble audience seems to have little of the necessary imagination, for they violate the imaginative space of the play, which the players have first breached, by mocking the actors, laughing at their tragic efforts, and talking loudly among themselves during the performance. For them a play is only the means to while away a dull wait on their wedding night and, secure in an untroubled sense of their own substantial reality, they can laugh at what unrealistic and trivial things all plays and players are. Theseus, that champion of Athenian rationalism, has already publicly declared that the poet's imagination is no more truthful than the lunatic's delusions or the lover's belief in the perfect beauty of his beloved:

> The poet's eye, in a fine frenzy rolling,
> Doth glance from heaven to earth, from earth to heaven;
> And as imagination bodies forth
> The forms of things unknown, the poet's pen
> Turns them to shapes, and gives to airy nothing
> A local habitation and a name

(5.1.12–17)

Shakespeare seems to have constructed in *Dream* the "worst case" for theater, voicing all the attacks on drama being made in his time and deliberately showing plays, actors, and audiences at their worst. And since "the best in this kind are but shadows," *Pyramus and Thisbe* seems to indict all plays, including *A Midsummer Night's Dream*, as mere rant of awkward actors and unrealistic dreaming of frenzied poets. But, while admitting the worst, Shakespeare has contrived at the same time to defend plays in a most subtle fashion. Even as Theseus and his friends sit watching *Pyramus and Thisbe,* laughing at poetry and plays and actors, they are themselves, seen from our vantage point in the outer audience, only the "forms of things unknown" which the imagination of William Shakespeare bodied forth and gave the habitation of Athens and such odd names as Helena and Hermia, Demetrius and Lysander. The situation is the same as that in *Love's Labour's Lost,* where the scorn for plays is also discredited by showing the audience to be themselves only players, and not such very good ones at that, in a larger play of which they are totally unaware.

This is true in *Dream* in the literal sense that the stage audience is made up of actors in Shakespeare's play, and also in the sense that they have already been unwitting players in another internal play written and produced by that master of illusion, Oberon, king of the fairies. He and Titania between them have earlier managed the lives of Theseus and Hippolyta as if they were unconscious actors in a play, and during the course of *Dream*, Oberon contrives on the stage of his magical forest a little illusion which instructs the young lovers, feelingly not consciously, in the dangers of unleashed passion and brings them at last to a happy conclusion in which every Jack has his Jill. Oberon's magical forest is a perfect image of what a theater might ideally be and do, but even here the most all-powerful of playwrights is subject to the ability of the imperfect instruments through whom he must implement his art, and Puck nearly ruins the play by putting "idleness" in the wrong eyes.

As we in the audience watch Theseus watching Bottom pretend to be Pyramus, the extended dramatic perspective forces us to consider the possibility that we too may be only another player audience on another larger stage. And if this is the case, then the audience is not only once again reminded by the bad manners of the stage audience of the positive part it must play in making theater work, but it is also being told than its own sense of the real may be no more valid than Theseus's. If his rationalistic scorn of plays and players is called into question by his status as only another player, then perhaps our skepticism about Shakespeare's play is equally compromised, for we stand in the same relationship to the things unknown that the imagination of William Shakespeare has bodied forth as *A Midsummer Night's Dream* as Theseus does to *Pyramus and Thisbe*. A forest ruled over by a contentious fairy king and queen, a magical love potion which causes love at first sight, a comic trickster like Puck, all are at least as real as a player duke who marries a queen of Amazons, rules over a city named Athens, and believes that a way of thinking called reason shows the truth of things. And they may finally be as real as that "sure and firm-set earth" we take to be our own reality. If *all* the world is a play, then one play may be as true as another; and if the conditions are right, as in Oberon's play but not in Bottom's, then the theater may reveal the true nature of the world and effect its transformation.

The playwright drives home his point in the final scene. After Theseus and Hippolyta and the other couples, Bottom's play finished, make their way to bed thinking that reality reigns again, the stage fills with all those fairies which Shakespeare's imagination created to embody his vision of the beneficent but tricky forces at work in nature, just beyond the range of the daylight eye. Again it is done lightly, the claim half concealed and discounted even as it is so charmingly made, but immediate reality is being heavily discounted and a visionary power is being claimed for the dramatic poet by leaving his fairies in possession of a stage which now extends outward to claim the entire theater and the world beyond as a part of its imaginative realm.

In *Dream* Shakespeare claims for the dramatic poet all the powers which the Renaissance conferred on art, but his image of the theater still acknowledges the crudity and accidents of stage presentation, the clumsiness of actors, the incomprehension of audiences, and the danger that plays may be mere fantasy without much relation to reality. If the play is to work, as he tries to make *Dream* work, and its full powers are to be realized, then actors and audience must accept that they and their "real" world are finally as illusory as a play, are simply another play called reality, and enter with their imaginations into the full spirit of creating between them on the stage an alternate fictional world of faires and lovers which can reveal another aspect of truth.

In Shakespeare's exploration of theater in his plays of the 1590s, the poet-playwright does not himself appear openly but only in some surrogate form of creator such as the Prince of Navarre and his companions, who construct an academy and a masque; or Petruchio, who writes his shrew play as he goes along; or Oberon, who commands the illusory power of the fairy world; or perhaps even the enthusiastic actor Bottom, who is always willing to stretch a part or add a piece of business to the script of the mercifully anonymous *Pyramus.* The absence of any direct image of the playwright accords with the actual situation in the public theater, where the playwright and his text remained invisible behind the production of the play. It was the play in performance in the theater before an audience that was the artistic reality, and it is on production that Shakespeare focused his attention in his internal plays, showing always in these early plays a less than ideal situation.

It may be, of course, that in treating the theater in its negative aspects, concentrating on its problems while only implying its successes, Shakespeare was calling attention by contrast to the effectiveness of his own plays and their productions, in which he participated as an actor. He was, after all, a professional writer for what was by all accounts a skillful professional company playing in an excellent London theater, while the players he portrays in his plays are either members of a touring road company or amateurs performing old-fashioned entertainments and dramatizations of "moldy tales" in a pavilion in an open park, the dining hall of a great house, and the presence chamber of a court. No doubt there was some of a professional's feeling of superiority to the amateur in all of this, but these theatrical situations also image, in however indirect or exaggerated a way, the public theater for which Shakespeare wrote. And they make it clear that Shakespeare was profoundly sensitive to the fact that the wrong kind of actors, productions, and audiences could destroy a play, no matter how good the text itself might be.

About the power of plays themselves and their potentially beneficial effects on life, he seems to have been at this time highly optimistic and to have felt that the playwright was not a mere entertainer but a dramatic poet. Playing of the right kind could transform Sly from a tinker to a lord and Kate from a shrew into a loving wife, and at the same time be not merely the image of such transformations but the means by which they might be achieved. In *Love's Labour's Lost,* though frustrated in actual performance, art in all forms including the play has the potential for uniting a variety of people, men and women, nobles and commoners, and adjusting their natural conflicts in such a way as to bring them to a happy ending and provide them with the fame or love they seek. In *Dream* we see the success of art in the world of the fairies where Oberon creates illusions and directs a plot which undoes the tangles and dissolves the hatred and frustration of the young lovers. It is important to note that in these plays art is never seen as some abstract thing far removed from life but always as a force working directly and immediately upon life, changing the world by reconciling opposites and transmuting a difficult reality into the forms that man desires.

But despite the high potentials of playing, it either never quite works in these plays, or it works against odds. The actors are often "o'erparted," like the Prince of Navarre and his companions, or the "Nine Worthies," or Bottom's company, taking on high heroic roles which strain nature and for which their talents are inadequate. Or they are motivated in wrong ways which eventually lead to a bad performance, as Petruchio's greed leads him to overplaying his swaggering style and finally being outplayed by Kate, or as Bottom's bumptious and ill-placed confidence in his histrionic powers makes him want to absorb *all* the parts in the play—"Let me play the lion too"—and leads to him overreaching himself in "a part to tear a cat in." Performances can also be spoiled by actors like Kate as she first appears, or the prince and his companions, or the young lovers, all of whom have too little sense of themselves as actors and play out their parts without any understanding of their status as players. The danger is always a performance like *Pyramus and Thisbe,* in which imagination and reality are not sufficiently balanced to create the illusion a successful play requires to work its magic. The ideal seems to be a performance in which reality is neither so openly flouted as to make the play unbelievable, nor rendered so literally as to make it ridiculous, but is balanced with imaginative pretense in such a way as to manifest the purpose of playing itself, the channeling of nature by art into harmonious and satisfactory patterns.

The audiences bear as much responsibility as the players for creating this ideal, and they fail to play their parts as regularly as do the actors. Occasionally they may be taken in and believe in the illusion too completely, as Sly does in believing that he *is* a lord, or Bottom in believing that he is an ass beloved by the queen of fairies. But most often it is an imaginatively deficient audience in these early plays which contributes to the failure of performances by refusing to enter into the necessary pretense. Reality is too real for them, and so the young ladies in *Love's Labour's Lost* will not forget for the moment that the young men in the masque are really only clumsy lovers who a moment ago were pretending to be philosophers. So, too, the audiences at the *Pageant of the Nine Worthies* and *Pyramus and Thisbe* lack the imagination to understand that they too are actors, and not such good ones, and they therefore do not show the necessary good manners and courtesy which would help to overcome the ineptitude of the actors and make the play a success. Their jeers and mockery not only fluster and discourage the actors but invade and destroy the magical space of the stage where the fragile but powerful illusion of art must work.

Fancy's Images

Ruth Nevo

"*A Midsummer Night's Dream* is best seen," says G. K. Hunter, "as a lyric divertissement . . . Shakespeare has lavished his art on the separate excellencies of the different parts, but has not sought to show them growing out of one another in a process analogous to that of symphonic 'development.'" I would claim, on the contrary, symphonic development of a particularly subtle kind; both itself an impressive achievement in the unifying of complexities, and a distinct conquest in the zig-zag progress towards Shakespeare's comic paradigm. This is a highly intellectual, highly speculative comedy, like *Love's Labour's Lost* not the refashioning of a previously-treated story or play but an original invention. Through his basic comic structure of initial privation or perversity, comic device both deceptive and remedial, knots of errors and final recognitions, Shakespeare has achieved not only a benign resolution to the dialectic of folly and wisdom, but a complex and witty exploration of the infirmities and frailties and deficiencies and possibilities of the imaginative faculty itself.

The problem presented to Theseus four days before his wedding is a knotty one. From the point of view of the father, what is required is that his daughter yield to his bidding and accept the suitor he has approved. But this would please no one but himself (and Demetrius). Theseus adopts the patriarchal view, naturally enough. But suppose (in another age and another clime) the young people had been left to choose their own mates? This procedure would not have solved the

From *Comic Transformations in Shakespeare*. © 1980 by Ruth Nevo. Methuen, 1980.

problem any more satisfactorily than the first, since the predicament we are asked to take in consists precisely of the asymmetry in the feelings of these four young people. The father's peremptoriness and the Duke's supportive edict lend urgency to their problem, but do not create it. The initial presentation of the situation invites us to perceive that while the tyrannical *senex* provides the outward and immediate obstacle to be surmounted, the root of the problem is elsewhere and within. The initiating recalcitrancy is the fact that two young men are competing with each other for one girl, when there is another available, and willing, to turn a triangle into a suitable set of couples. Two of both kinds makes up four, as Puck succinctly expresses it. And, it seems, some such arrangement had once been contemplated by these young Athenians themselves. Lysander (and later Helena) tells us that Demetrius made love to Helena before obtaining Egeus's consent to a match with Hermia. He deserted her then, it seems, for Hermia. But why? And when? "This man," says Egeus (of Demetrius) "hath my consent to marry her" (Hermia). "This man" (of Lysander), "hath bewitch'd the bosom of my child." But it is impossible to determine the sequence of tenses. Did the bewitching occur before the consent, or since, or simultaneously? Was it perhaps some sudden new interest in Hermia on the part of Demetrius that stimulated Lysander's desire for her? Or could it possibly be a case of the other foot? Did Lysander's interest in Hermia deflect Demetrius's previous affection for Helena and draw it with magnetic attraction towards the object of Lysander's love?

The square-dance view of these proceedings is less helpful than it seems, mainly because it takes no account of the girls. "The lovers are like dancers," says G. K. Hunter, "who change partners in the middle of a figure; the point at which partners are exchanged is determined by the dance, the pattern, and not by the psychological state of the dancers." But we are asked to attend quite closely to "the psychological state of the dancers," to the "fierce vexations" of their dream. The girls, in point of fact, do not change partners at all. They are subjected to drastic changes in their lovers' attitudes, to which they bewilderedly respond, but their own attachments do not waver. Moreover, the play's peripeteia is a comic reversal which leaves in effect everything exactly where it was: Puck's mistake with the magic juice—designed by Oberon to rectify unrequited love—in fact compounds error and disturbance by causing the two young men to continue to be both in love with the same love object, though this time in the shape of the other girl. It is thus not a question of mistaken identity, or of disguise, those time-honoured sources of identity confusion in New Comedy plots. Nor it is quite true to say, though it is often said, that the lovers simply don't know what they want, are fickle, capricious and unreasonable, creatures of the senses, of the eye merely. It is worth attending to Helena's observations at the play's outset:

> How happy some o'er other some can be!
> Through Athens I am thought as fair as she.
> But what of that? Demetrius thinks not so;
> He will not know what all but he do know;
> And as he errs, doting on Hermia's eyes,
> So I, admiring of his qualities.
> Things base and vile, holding no quantity,
> Love can transpose to form and dignity.
> Love looks not with the eyes but with the mind;
> And therefore is wing'd Cupid painted blind.
> Nor hath Love's mind of any judgment taste;
> Wings, and no eyes, figure unheedy haste;
> And therefore is Love said to be a child,
> Because in choice he is so oft beguil'd.
> As waggish boys in game themselves forswear,
> So the boy Love is perjur'd every where;
> For ere Demetrius look'd on Hermia's eyne,
> He hail'd down oaths that he was only mine;
> And when this hail some heat from Hermia felt,
> So he dissolv'd, and show'rs of oaths did melt.
>
> (1.1.226–45)

If only Demetrius would use his eyes she says in effect, he would see that I am as fair as Hermia. If Demetrius' infected will did not betray him he would recognize this open and palpable truth. But if Helena and Hermia are identical in this cardinal matter of their beauty, then there are no visual grounds for preference either way, and therefore there can be no question of errors in choice. Helena intelligently perceives this catch and she also perceives that what is sauce for the goose is sauce for the gander. "So I" (err), she says, "admiring in *his* qualities." Helena announces with bitterness this insight concerning the total and wayward non-dependence of erotic preference upon visual perception: "Love looks not with the eyes but with the mind; / And therefore is wing'd Cupid painted blind." The comedy of the speech lies, of course, in Helena's asumption that "eyes" offer a more objective basis for judgment in love than mind. Eyes don't indeed provide any security for love, nor any true representation of reality, as the woods prove; but then neither does (rational) mind. Later the be-witched Lysander's assertion that "the will of man is by his reason sway'd; / And reason says you are the worthier maid" will be suffi-cient evidence of that. Helena's "mind" is Desdemona's: "I saw Othello's visage in his mind" (1.3.252) and Othello's: "I therefore beg it not . . . But to be free and bounteous to her mind" (1.3.–265). Only there (tragically) and here (comically) the mind, that subjective source of value, of form and of dignity, is subject to all kinds of disabilities and derange-ments. Mind, in its aspect as the image-making and image-perceiving faculty, is an errant faculty indeed, unstable, uncertain, wavering, and seeking anchorage among a welter of rival images and self-images. It is to these, I believe, that the opening of the play draws our attention.

What we are invited to perceive is a falling out among rivals, and what we are invited to infer is that, at a deeper psychic level than they are aware of, they do indeed know what they want: each wants what his brother-at-arms or rival has. We have the case of Proteus and Valentine for confirmation of Shakespeare's interest in the phenome-non. Says Proteus, with admirable candour:

> Even as one heat another heat expels,
> Or as one nail by strength drives out another,
> So the remembrance of my former love
> Is by a newer object quite forgotten.
> [Is it] mine [eye], or Valentinus' praise,
> Her true perfection, or my false transgression,
> That makes me, reasonless, to reason thus?
>
> (2.4.192–98)

Consider the extremely provoking nature of Lysander's remark to Demetrius:

> You have her father's love, Demetrius,
> Let me have Hermia's; do you marry *him*
>
> (my italics; 1.1.93–94)

Consider too the amplitude and intensity with which the sisterly affection between the two girls is treated:

> all the counsel that we two have shar'd,
> The sister's vows, the hours that we have spent

· · · · · · · · · · · · · · ·

> All school-day's friendship, childhood innocence
>
> . . . .
>
> Both on one sampler, sitting on one cushion,
> Both warbling of one song, both in one key
>
> . . . .
>
>   So we grew together,
> Like to a double cherry.
>
>   (3.2. 198–209 passim)

It furthermore transpires, as the play winds deeper into its conflicts in act 2, that Oberon and Titania are also at odds over a love object they both want. The competitive marital duel of this couple features antecedent jealousies, but at the moment in time the play dramatizes they are quarrelling over possession of the changeling child. We find immediate parodic confirmation of the incidence of this malady as early as act 1, scene 2, where the good Bottom, magnifier of folly, wants to play all the parts Peter Quince distributes to his cast—tyrants, lovers, ladies and lions—and is in his comic hubris convinced that he can do better at them all than any of his fellows.

Rivalry, then, fraternal or quasi-sibling, or marital is the comic disposition which the comic device exposes and exacerbates. It is also worth noting that the story of the night is set within a frame of *concordia discors* between erstwhile military rivals. Theseus wooed Hippolyta, we learn, with his sword, and won her love doing her injuries. This reconciliatory *concordia discors* is symbolized in the description of the hunt in act 4, scene 1, just before the royal pair discovers the one time "rival enemies" now "new in amity." Theseus invites his Queen to the mountain top to

> mark the musical confusion
> Of hounds and echo in conjunction
>   (4.1.110–11)

and she, remembering the hounds of Sparta, transforms his notion of dissonant confusion into the perception of a higher harmony:

>   Never did I hear
> Such gallant chiding; for besides the groves,
> The skies, the fountains, every region near
> Seem all one mutual cry. I never heard
> So musical a discord, such sweet thunder.
>   (4.1.114–18)

Hippolyta is consistently Theseus's informant in the play and indeed Egeus might have done well to appeal to her judgment rather than his at the beginning. Fortunately, however, for what the play enables us to discover about rivalries, he did not. Rivalry is benign when it leads to differentiation, since concord rquires distinct entities between which to exist; and harmful when it leads to the blurring of boundaries, to "unnatural" imitative, or confusing conjunctions. Hippolyta is no longer playing the role of a man-woman Amazon by this time. The play explores the comedy of mimicry in four different and complementary perspectives—that of the quasi-fraternal lovers, the quasi-sibling "sisters," the Fairy Queen and her votaress, and the amateur comedians, the artisans of Athens, with the putative arch-mimic Bottom, who is never anything but himself, at their head.

Sibling rivalry takes the form of unconscious mimicry, an identification with the brother who must therefore be outdone in *his* sphere. I am as good as he. I am better than he. I must have what he has. "I am, my lord as well deriv'd as he, / As well possess'd," says Lysander, and what is more, beloved of beauteous Hermia. And Demetrius later: "I love thee more than he can do." From the girls' side of the picture we have Helena: "Through Athens I am thought as fair as she." Sensible siblings fight their way into maturity by seeking, finding, exploiting, inventing if necessary, precisely those differences and distinctions between them which establish their individual identities, on the basis of which they can freely choose their mates. This is no doubt why identical twins are such a problem, and so disturbing we are told, to the primitive mind encountering sameness where difference is not only in order, is not only expected, but is indispensable to individuation. But identical twins are an accident of nature which the comic artist may exploit for errors, if he wishes. What we have in *Midsummer Night's Dream* is imagined identical twinship. It is just such an idealized childhood twinship that Helena invokes in her remonstrance to Hermia over the latter's treacherous confederacy (as she believes) with the men, both now in pursuit of her to mock her:

> Is all the counsel that we two have shar'd,
> The sisters' vows, the hours that we have spent,
> When we have chid the hasty-footed time
> For parting us—O, is all forgot?
> All school-days' friendship, childhood innocence?
> We, Hermia, like two artificial gods,

Have with our needles created both one flower,
Both on one sampler, sitting on one cushion,
Both warbling of one song, both in one key,
As if our hands, our sides, voices, and minds
Had been incorporate. So we grew together,
Like to a double cherry, seeming parted,
But yet an union in partition,
Two lovely berries moulded on one stem;
So, with two seeming bodies, but one heart,

. . . .

And will you rent our ancient love asunder,
To join with men in scorning your poor friend?
                              (3.2.198–212; 215–16)

A replica of such an "incorporation" at a later and more complex
stage of a woman's life is Titania's relationship with her favourite
votaress. Titania's account of her friendship with the boy's mother
contains a wonderfully articulated image of imaginative mimicry:

His mother was a vot'ress of my order.
And in the spiced Indian air, by night,
Full often hath she gossip'd by my side,
And sat with me on Neptune's yellow sands,
Marking th' embarked traders on the flood;
When we have laugh'd to see the sails conceive
And grow big-bellied with the wanton wind;
Which she, with pretty and with swimming gait,
Following (her womb then rich with my young squire)
Would imitate, and sail upon the land
To fetch me trifles, and return again,
As from a voyage, rich with merchandise.

                              (2.1. 123–34)

Peter Quince's troupe literalize metaphors, too, but here the Indian
maid's imitation of the big-bellied sails has a function other than
reductio ad absurdum. The friends share the playful vision of the billow-
ing sails as pregnant, which the expectant mother then playfully mimes,
for the amusement and gratification of her companion. What is rendered here, we are invited to infer, is a vividly emphathetic, imaginative sharing of the experience of pregnancy; and therefore when the
mother dies it is no wonder that Titania's attachment to the child is

more than the charitable rearing of an orphan. "And for her sake do I rear up her boy: / And for her sake I will not part with him" has the ring of self-justification—she is claiming nothing for this adoption but an act of conventional piety—but what we see is that she has so identified herself with her votaress that the child has become her own. Oberon, furiously observing his exclusion from this relationship, wants to possess himself of the love object she is so wrapped up in, and, failing, will punish her by caricaturing her defection. She is to dote upon the first living creature she sees:

> (Be it on lion, bear, or wolf, or bull,
> On meddling monkey, or on busy ape),
> (2.1.180–81)

The animus, however, of

> Set your heart at rest;
> The fairy land buys not the child of me.
> (2.1.121–22)

invites us to infer (especially if we remember "childing" autumn in her description of the disordered and distemperatured seasons) that Oberon might mend his marriage more effectively by getting Titania with child than by trying to get Titania without child. But rivalry and revenge (for previous peccadilloes real or imagined, with Theseus and Hippolyta) is the order of the day at this stage—a midsummer madness—of the battle of the sexes, and at this stage of the comic development, which is the laying bare of the particular comic disposition dominant in the play.

The double plotting of *A Midsummer Night's Dream* is superb because it is so subtly related. Marital rivalry is more complex because double-decked: marriage partners must maintain their distinctive personalities, recognize each other's and enter into a new corporate personality, or transaction of personalities. But in this marriage on the rocks, with Titania playing the part of imagined twin to her votaress, and Oberon competing with her for possession of the Indian boy, rivalry has taken the place of reciprocity, competition of co-operation, and a riotous mimicry of clearly differentiated sexual roles.

We begin to perceive the nature of the comic infirmity in *A Midsummer Night's Dream*. It is that fluidity and instability of imagination which causes an individual to be either too identified or not identified enough; to resemble when to discriminate would be more politic and more appropriate; to represent reality in images generated by the desires of the mind.

Nature spirits that they are, these fairies, nature perfectly reflects their marital dissensions:

> Therefore the winds
>
> . . . .
>
> As in revenge, have suck'd up from the sea
> Contagious fogs; which, falling in the land,
> Hath every pelting river made so proud
> That they have overborne their continents
>
> . . . .
>
>   and the green corn
> Hath rotted ere his youth attain'd a beard
>
> . . . .
>
> The nine men's morris is fill'd up with mud,
> And the quaint mazes in the wanton green,
> For lack of tread, are undistinguishable
>
> . . . .
>
>   hoary-headed frosts
> Fall in the fresh lap of the crimson rose,
> And on old Heims' [thin] and icy crown
> An odorous chaplet of sweet summer buds
> Is, as in mockery, set; the spring, the summer,
> The childing autumn, angry winter, change
> Their wonted liveries; and the mazed world,
> By their increase, now knows not which is which.
>
>   (2.1.88–114 passim)

"Undistinguishability" and the wilder follies of not knowing which is which receive their richest comic gloss from the good artisans of Athens in their entanglement with the problems of dramatic representation—when a wall is a wall for example, or a lion Snug the Joiner; but the message of this *paysage moralisé* is quite clear: confusion, disorder, disarray, mock mimicry reign in the woods, and with all distinction gone, all relations are perverse or fruitless or unnatural. Puck's mischievous translation of Bottom literally embodies asininity. But it also reflects Titania's wrong-headed "incorporation" of the Indian boy. It is a bonus for Oberon's punitive plan (he did not envisage monsters), while the metamorphosis and the coupling of Titania with this comic monster inflates the folly of misconceived images *ad absurdum*, revealing (but not to the victims) truth in motley.

The strategy of comedy is to maximalize error before matters will mend; the maximalizing indeed generates the mending. To Helena there does come a glimmer of liberating wisdom in the woods when she says: "What wicked and dissembling glass of mine / Made me compare with Hermia's sphery eyne?' (2.2.98–99). This anticipates remedy but is as yet in too self-abasing a form. The *processus turbarum*, with its cumulative and preposterous turbulence brings about for the lovers an intensification of folly to the point of giddying exhaustion; and discernment—the wisdom of discrimination, of getting images right—will emerge from the chaos, or de-composition of topsy-turvydom.

There should be no expounding of dreams, as Bottom knows, but the magic juice applied to sleeping eyes—the comic device—reveals in this play its fully Shakespearean iridescence. It is both delusive and applied in error and so causes the knot of errors and perturbations; but it is also the cause of ultimate reclamation and recognition. The magic at work operates therapeutically, cathartically, like dreams indeed. It discovers, enlarging as in a distorting mirror, the shadowy wishes and fears of the mind, and by so doing enables the victims to enfranchize themselves from their obsessions. Shakespeare's moonlit wood, alive with trolls, grotesques and ambivalence is a potent symbol for the creative subconscious. And Puck, conveyor of dreams and potions, impish homogenizer, can be seen as a genius of comedy itself, mimicking (in the likeness of a filly foal, or a roasted crab), mocking, decreating as he gives all nature's ingredients a great stir. As does Bottom, counterpoint Buffoon to Puck's Eiron (and unwitting Impostor as Titania's lover), giving all the theatre's ingredients a great stir:

> Nay; you must name his name, and half his face must be seen through the lion's neck, and he himself must speak through, saying thus, or to the same defect: . . . my life for yours. If you think I come hither as a lion, it were pity of my life.
>
> (3.2.36–43)

Puck's error—to him all Athenians are alike—is homeopathic. It reflects the comic disposition of the play, exposes it, and is exactly what is required to exacerbate and exorcise it.

Thus, so far from the warblings of one song in one key, the fierce vexations of misprision in act 3 bring about a positively inflamed consciousness of difference: " 'Little' again? Nothing but 'low' and 'little'?" Abuse and vilification are not lacking on all sides: "Thou cat, thou bur! Vile thing . . . tawny Tartar . . . loathed medicine" are a string of epithets from a sometime lover sufficient to draw from Hermia (to Helena) "You juggler! You canker-blossom! You thief of love!" For which she gets as good as she gives with Helena's "Fie, fie, you counterfeit, you puppet, you!" " 'Puppet'?" shouts Hermia at this point:

> Ay, that way goes the game.
> Now I perceive that she hath made compare
> Between our statures: she hath urg'd her height,
> And with her personage, her tall personage,
> Her height, forsooth, she hath prevail'd with him.
> And are you grown so high in his esteem,
> Because I am so dwarfish and so low?
> How low am I, thou painted maypole? Speak!
> How low am I? I am not yet so low
> But that my nails can reach unto thine eyes.
>   (3.2.289–98)

"O, when she is angry," retorts a onetime part of an incorporate double cherry,

> she is keen and shrewd!
> She was a vixen when she went to school;
> And though she be but little, she is fierce.
>   (3.2.323–35)

This knot of errors is the world upside down, and Helena's idyllic and lost childhood "incorporation" is well and truly mocked, as are Lysander's protestations of love to Hermia when transposed to

> Get you gone, you dwarf;
> You minimus, of hind'ring knot-grass made;
> You bead, you acorn.
>   (3.2.328–30)

At the same time these frenetic hyperboles are the fulfilment and the acting out of everyone's deepest anxieties, misgivings and obsessions. Hermia foresaw all and foresuffered all when she dreamt of Lysander watching a serpent eating her heart away, and Helena's masochism—

her seeking to "enrich her pain"—to cause the pain she dreads and loves—has progressed from her embracing of the role of fawning and beaten spaniel (1.1.246–51) to a paroxysm of self-abasement: "No, no; I am as ugly as a bear" (2.2.94). And this even before she becomes convinced of her victimization at the hand of all.

The *processus turbarum* of act 3, by intensifying aberration and detonating hidden psychic dynamite discomposes, disorients and disintegrates. They all collapse in the end, exhausted by these traumas and by the hectic pursuit through the woods, and when they awake they are tranquil and clear-seeing. Now that vision is improved they are able to look back upon their "dream" experience as upon something distant and blurred. Hermia says: "Methinks I see these things with parted eye, / When every thing seems double", and Helena concurs: "So methinks; / And I have found Demetrius like a jewel, / Mine own, and not mine own" (4.1.189–92). These are pregnant sayings, these musings of the wondering and half-enlightened lovers. Perception and self-perception have passed through the alembic of dream and have been catalyzed. Demetrius, now seeing his love for Hermia as a childhood gaud and Helena as once again "the object and the pleasure of (his) eye" speaks for all four when he says:

These things seem small and undistinguishable,
Like far-off mountains turned into clouds.

(4.1.187–88)

It is an interesting word "undistinguishable." And it occurs only once again in Shakespeare: in Titania's description of confusion and disorder in nature already quoted.

The formal remedy, as Puck himself calls it, of the play is purely ophthalmic. Oberon's corrective juice causes the lovers when they awake from their sleep to sort themselves out into suitable couples— Jacks and Jills, as Puck puts it with benign contempt—and Titania to be released from her unsuitable coupling with sweet bully Bottom. But the whole question of corrected vision, of the tutored imagination, goes beyond the merely technical exigencies of plot. It is the essential mediator of the benign, non-disjunctive dialectic which conjures rejoicing out of mockery, and wisdom out of folly.

In the lovers' case errors of "vision" are removed so that true relations can be re-discerned. The lovers recuperate, literally, from their "trip." Lysander, it is now clear, fell into an infatuation with Helena when he was really in love with Hermia, and Demetrius fell into an infatuation with Hermia when he was really in love with Helena. But in the fairies' case, Titania, chastened by the onslaughts of the tender passion, relinquishes the child; and this yielding to Oberon's will produces in him the impulse of compassion required to melt hard-heartedness, soften anger and renounce retaliation. The passage is worth particular attention:

> Her dotage now I do begin to pity.
> For meeting her of late behind the wood,
> Seeking sweet favors for this hateful fool,
> I did upbraid her, and fall out with her.
> For she his hairy temples then had rounded
> With coronet of fresh and fragrant flowers;
> And that same dew which sometime on the buds
> Was wont to swell like round and orient pearls,
> Stood now within the pretty flouriets' eyes,
> Like tears that did their own disgrace bewail.
> When I had at my pleasure taunted her,
> And she in mild terms begg'd my patience,
> I then did ask of her her changeling child;
> Which straight she gave me, and her fairy sent
> To bear him to my bower in fairy land.
> And now I have the boy, I will undo
> This hateful imperfection of her eyes.
>
> (4.1.47–63)

In this recognition scene Oberon sees her, perhaps for the first time, certainly for the first time since "Ill met by moonlight, proud Titania" in act 2, with detachment and tenderness.

Eyes are organs of visions; eyes (especially when starry) are beautiful objects of vision. But eyes are also vessels for tears. Titania's amorous fantasy as she orders Bottom led away to her bower will be recalled:

> The moon methinks looks with a wat'ry eye;
> And when she weeps, weeps every little flower,
> Lamenting some enforced chastity.
>
> (3.2.198–200)

Drugs, potions, condiments alter vision and visibility, but the true transfigurations are those which take place invisibly at the heart. Bottom himself makes this point, as modestly as ever. When told by Peter

Quince that Pyramus had been a lover "that kills himself most gallant for love," "That," remarks the sage Bottom, "will ask some tears in the true performing of it. If I do it, let the audience look to their eyes."

A Midsummer Night's Dream juggles conspicuously with multiple levels of representation, with plays-within-plays and visions within dreams. What is performed, what is meant, what is seen are often, as Theseus said of Peter Quince's prologue "like a tangled chain; nothing impair'd, but all disorder'd" (5.1.125–26). The Athenian lovers, Lysander and Hermia, fall asleep and dream (in act 2), fall asleep and wake (in act 4), and what happens to them is ambiguously dream/reality, just as Oberon king of shadows, is ambiguously real/not real, visible to the audience but not to the lovers; and the "angel" that wakes Titania "from her flow'ry bed" (3.1.129) is visible to her but not to the audience, who perceive only Nick Bottom assified. Puck stage-manages these "transfigurations" for Oberon's delectation just as Peter Quince does for Theseus' and Shakespeare for ours. And the audience is more than once pointedly invited to conflate these frames. When Theseus says "The best in this kind are but shadows," his remark applies with equal validity to the artisans of Athens and the Lord Chamberlain's Men. By the same token Puck's "shadows" in the epilogue ("if we shadows have offended") refers, intentionally, both to the fairies and the actors—the visible and the invisible.

Act 5 dazzlingly catches up and re-focuses the issues of the play, recapitulating its schooling of the imagination. When Theseus tempers Hippolyta's impatience with the mechanicals' efforts: "This is the silliest stuff that ever I heard" (5.1.210) with "The best in this kind are but shadows; and the worst are no worse, if imagination amend them" (5.1.211–12) he is retracting his previous repudiation of the imagination as the faculty which "sees more devils than vast hell can hold," or "Helen's beauty in a brow of Egypt," or some bringer of what is a merely "apprehended" joy, or a bear in a bush on a dark night. The rationalistic and empirically minded duke has been more than cautious about the seething tricks of that fertile and moonstruck faculty; and it is in reply to his dismissal of the lovers' story as so much irrational and illusory dream stuff that Hippolyta enters her caveat concerning the story of the night:

> But all the story of the night told over,
> And all their minds transfigur'd so together,
> More witnesseth than fancy's images,
> And grows to something of great constancy
> (5.1. 23–26)

The ducal pair, as we have seen, are a model of *concordia discors* ("How shall we find the concord of this discord?" Theseus asks of the "very tragical mirth" about to be presented by the artisans) and so it is fitting that they should conduct the dialectic of real and imaginary, meant and performed, visible and invisible towards a resolution for theatre-goers and lovers alike. When Hippolyta reflects upon the story of the night, she is inviting not only Theseus but the theatre audience as well to further reflection. She is inviting a retrospective reappraisal of all that has been enacted in the moonlit woods. Hippolyta's organic metaphor is interesting; cognition, it says, or re-cognition, grows in the mind in the process of recounting, re-telling. What the play celebrates as remedial, beneficent, recuperative it will have discovered by working its way through the fantastic follies the initial deficiencies or infirmities generated. These follies, reduced (or expanded) to absurdity, will prove to have been homeopathically therapeutic, if imagination amend them by making them intelligible. "It must be your imagination then, not theirs," says wise Hippolyta, knowing that to stout bully Bottom nothing is invisible, not even a voice from behind a wall. So far as that parodic literalist of the imagination is concerned, moonlight cannot be better represented than by moonlight, shining in at the casement in all its factual actuality. And when a person is a wall, he must be well and truly plastered and roughcast. No fancy Brechtian placards will do for him, any more than he can conceive that anyone (of any size) called Mustardseed should not be instantly applied to roast beef.

Pyramus and Thisbe presents a tragedy of lovers misprisions, and neutralizes disaster with its ludicrous comicality. It is irresistibly amusing in itself and needs no amending, by imagination or any other means; and it is also the vehicle of Shakespeare's most ironic private joke to *his* audience over the heads, so to speak, of Peter Quince and his. The latter possess the capacity to distinguish between walls and witty partitions, between run-on and end-stopped pentameters, between a lion and a goose and between a man and a moon. But they haven't always been so good at distinguishing. Their own follies have been, in their own way, no less de-constructive; but also no less recreative.

"Your play needs no excuse," says Theseus, amused, ironic and kind. "Marry, if he that writ it had play'd Pyramus, and hang'd himself in Thisby's garter, it would have been a fine tragedy; and so it is truly, and very notably discharg'd" (5.1.357–61). A great deal, and of great constancy, has been "discharged" in this play. And not only

Hippolyta, it has been suggested, has had an inkling that the fantasy of folly may grow into the wisdom of the imagination.

This resonant insight marks, at the level of overt theme, the dramatic growth in *A Midsummer Night's Dream* of the dramatist's capacity to conceive and render the interlacing of sexual and individual roles. Further growth will issue, in due course, in the achievement of a comic form completely adequate for the dialectical battle of sex and self, a form which will resolve the ambivalencies of that warfare's tamings and matings. Here the idea is still inchoate, for it lacks as yet the crystallizing force of the heroine protagonist in all the fullness of her virtuosity and her autonomy.

The Bottom Translation

Jan Kott

QUINCE: *Bless thee, Bottom! Bless thee! Thou art translated.*

From Saturnalia to medieval *ludi* the ass is one of the main actors in processions, comic rituals, and holiday revels. In Bakhtin's succinct formula the ass is "the Gospel-symbol of debasement and humility (as well as concommitant regeneration)." On festive days such as the Twelfth Night, Plough Monday, the Feast of Fools, and the Feast of the Ass, merry and often vulgar parodies of liturgy were allowed. On those days devoted to general folly, clerics often participated as masters of ceremony, and an "Asinine Mass" was the main event. An ass was occasionally brought to the church, in which a hymn especially composed for the occasion would be sung:

> Orientis partibus
> Adventavit Asinus
> Pulcher et fortissimus
> Sarcinis aptissimus.

"Ass masses" were unknown in England, but the symbolism of the carnival ass and sacred *drolerie* survived from the Middle Ages until Elizabethan times. At the beginning of Elizabeth's reign donkeys dressed up as bishops or dogs with Hosts in their teeth would appear in court masques. But more significant than these animal disguises, which were a mockery of Catholic liturgy, was the appearance of the Bacchic

From *Assays: Critical Approaches to Medieval and Renaissance Texts*, vol. 1, edited by Peggy A. Knapp and Michael A. Stugrin. © 1981 by the University of Pittsburgh Press. The essay was translated by Daniela Miedzyrzecka.

73

donkey on stage. In Nashe's *Summer's Last Will and Testament,* performed in Croyden in 1592 or 1593, a few years before *A Midsummer Night's Dream,* Bacchus rode onto the stage atop an ass adorned wih ivy and garlands of grapes.

Among all festival masques of animals the figure of the ass is most polysemic. The icon of an ass, for Bakhtin "the most ancient and lasting symbol of the material bodily lower stratum," is the ritualistic and carnivalesque mediator between heaven and earth, which transforms the signs of the "top" into the signs of the "bottom." In its symbolic function of translation from the high to the low, the ass appears both in ancient tradition, in Apuleius, and in the Old and New Testament, as Balaam's she-ass who spoke in a human voice to give testimony to truth, and as the ass on which Jesus rode into Jerusalem for the last time. "Tell ye the daughter of Si-on, Behold thy King cometh unto thee, meek, and sitting upon an ass, and a colt foal of an ass" (Matt. 21.5).

The bodily meets with the spiritual in the *figura* and the masque of the ass. Therefore, the mating of Bottom and the Queen of the Fairies, which culminates the night and forest revelry, is so ambiguous and rich in meanings. In traditional interpretations of *A Midsummer Night's Dream,* the personae of the comedy belong to three different "worlds"; the court of Theseus and Hippolyta; the "Athenian" mechanicals; and the "supernatural" world of Oberon, Titania, and the "fairies." But particularly in this traditional interpretation, the night Titania spent with an ass in her "consecrated bower" must appear all the stranger and more unexpected.

Titania is the night double of Hippolyta, her dramatic and theatrical paradigm. Perhaps, since during the Elizabethan period the doubling of roles was very common, these two parts were performed by the same young boy. This Elizabethan convention was taken up by Peter Brook in his famous performance. But even if performed by different actors, Hippolyta's metamorphosis into Titania and her return to the previous state, like Theseus' transformation into Oberon, must have seemed much more obvious and natural to Elizabethan patrons than to audiences brought up on conventions of nineteenth- and twentieth-century theater. *A Midsummer Night's Dream* was most likely performed at an aristocratic wedding where court spectators knew the icons as well as the rules of a masque.

Court masques during the early Tudor and Elizabethan period were composed of three sequels: (1) appearance in mythological or shepherds' costumes; (2) dancing, occasionally with recitation or song; and (3) the ending of the masque, during which the masquers invited the court audience to participate in a general dance. Professional actors did not take part in masques, which were courtly masquerades and social games. "Going off" or "taking out," as this last dance was called, constituted the end of metamorphosis and a return of the masquers to their proper places and distinctions at court.

The disguises in the masque corresponded to social distinctions. The hierarchies were preserved. Dukes and lords would never consent to represent anyone below the mythological standing of Theseus. Theseus himself could only assume the shape of the "King of the Fairies" and Hippolyta, the "Queen of the Fairies." The annual Records at the Office of the Revels document the figures that appeared in court masques. Among fifteen sets of masking garments in 1555, there were "Venetian senators," "Venuses," "Huntresses," and "Nymphs." During the Jacobean period Nymphs of English rivers were added to the Amazons and Nymphs accompanying Diana, and Oberon with his knights was added to Acteon and his hunters. In 1611, nearly fifteen years after *A Midsummer Night's Dream,* young Henry, the king's son, appeared in the costume of the "faery Prince" in Jonson's *Oberon.*

The most frequent and popular figure of both courtly and wedding masque was Cupid. On a painting representing the wedding masque of Henry Unton in 1572, the guests seated at a table watch a procession of ten Cupids (five white ones and five black ones) accompanied by Mercury, Diana, and her six nymphs.

From the early Tudor masque to the sophisticated spectacles at the court of Inigo Jones, Cupid appears with golden wings, in the same attire, and with the same accessories: "a small boye to be cladd in a canvas hose and doblett sylverd over with a payre of winges of gold with bow and aroves, his eyes bended." This Cupid—with or without a blindfold—would randomly shoot his arrows at shepherdesses, sometimes missing:

> But I might see young Cupid's fiery shaft
> Quenched in the chaste beams of the watery moon;
> And the imperial votress passed on.

> (2.1.161–63)

But the Renaissance Cupid, who appears eight times in the poetic discourse of *A Midsummer Night's Dream,* has a different name, a different costume, and a different language as a person on stage. The blindfolded Cupid is "Anglicised" or "translated" into Puck, or Robin Goodfellow. On the oldest woodcut representing the folk Robin Goodfellow, in the 1628 story of his "Mad Pranks and Merry Jests," he holds in his right hand a large phallic candle and in his left hand a large broom. He has goat's horns on his head and goat's cloven feet. He is wearing only a skirt made of animal skins and is accompanied by black figures of men and women dressed in contemporary English garments and dancing in a circle. This "folk" Robin Goodfellow is still half a Satyr or Pan dancing with Nymphs.

The oldest image of Robin Goodfellow might refresh the imagination of scenographers and directors of A Midsummer Night's Dream who still see Puck as Romantic elf. But this engraving appears significant also for the interpretation of A Midsummer Night's Dream, where Shakespeare's wonderful syncretism mixes mythological icons of court masques with folk carnival. In A Midsummer Night's Dream mythological arrows are replaced by the folk love potion. In the poetic discourse this love potion still comes from the flower which turns red from Cupid's shaft. Shakespeare might have found the "love juice" in Montemayer's pastoral Diana, but he transposed the conventional simile into a sharp and brutal visual sign, the stage metaphor in which Puck sprays love juice in the eyes of the sleeping lovers.

"And maidens call it 'love-in-idleness' " (2.1.168). The flower's real name is pansy. Its other folk names are "Fancy," "Kiss me," "Cull me" or "Cuddle me to you," "Tickle my fancy," "Kiss me ere I arise," "Kiss me at the garden gate," and "Pink of my John." These are "bottom translations" of Cupid's shaft.

But in the discourse of A Midsummer Night's Dream there is not one flower, but two: "love-in-idleness" and its antidote. The opposition of "blind Cupid" and of Cupid with an "incorporeal eye" is translated into the opposition of mythic flowers: "Diana's bud o'er Cupid's flower / Hath ever such force and blessed power" (4.1.72–73)

The Neoplatonic unity of Love and Chastity is personified in the transformation of Venus into virginal Diana. Neoplatonists borrowed this exchange of signs from a line in Vergil's Aeneid, in which Venus appears to Aeneas as virginis arma: "on her shoulder she carried a bow as a huntress would" (1.327). In the semantics of emblems, the bow, weapon of Cupid-love, and the bow, weapon of Amazon-virgo, was a mediation between Venus and Diana. The harmony of the bow, as Plato called it, was for Pico "harmony in discord," a unity of opposites. From the union of Cupid and Psyche, brutally interrupted on

Earth, the daughter Voluptas was born in the heavens; from the adulterous relation of Mars and Venus, the daughter Harmony was born. Harmony, as Neoplatonists repeated after Ovid, Horace, and Plutarch, is *concordia discors* and *discordia concors*.

For Elizabethan poets and for carpenters who prepared court masques and entertainments, the exchange of icons and emblems became unexpectedly useful in the cult of the Virgin Queen. The transformation of Venus into Diana allowed them to praise Elizabeth simultaneously under the names of Cynthia/Diana and Venus, the goddess of love. In Paris's judgment, as Giordano Bruno explicated in *Eroici furori,* the apple awarded to the most beautiful goddess was symbolically given to the other two goddesses as well: "for in the simplicity of divine essence . . . all these perfections are equal because they are infinite."

George Peele must have read Bruno. In his *Arraignement of Paris,* the first extant English pastoral play with songs and dances by nymphs and shepherdesses, Paris hands the golden ball to Venus. When offended, Diana appeals to the gods on Olympus; the golden orb is finally delivered to Elizabeth, "queen of Second Troy." The nymph Elise is "Queen Juno's peer" and "Minerva's mate": As fair and lovely as the Queen of Love / As chaste as Dian in her chaste desires" (5.1.86–87).

In Ovid's *Metamorphoses,* "Titania" is one of Diana's names. Titania, in *A Midsummer Night's Dream,* appears without a bow. The bow is an emblem of the Queen of Amazons. In the first scene of act 1, Hippolyta in her first lines evokes the image of a bow: "And then the moon, like to a silver bow / Now-bent in heaven, shall behold the night / Of our solemnities" (1.1.9–11). Liturgical carnival starts with the new moon after the winter solstice. The new moon, like the letter D, resembles a strung bow. The moon, the "governess of floods" (2.1.103), is a sign of Titania; her nocturnal sports are "moonlight revels" (2.1.141). In the poetical discourse the bow of the Amazons and the bow of the moon relate Hippolyta and Titania.

A sophisticated game of the court, with allegorical eulogies and allusions, is played through the exchange of classical emblems later called "hieroglyphiches" by Ben Jonson. Greek Arcadia was slowly moving from Italy to England. Mythical figures and classical themes in masques, entertainments, and plays easily lent themselves to pastoral settings. But in this new pastoral mode the "Queen of the fairies" was still an allegory of Elizabeth. For the Entertainment of Elvetham behind the palace at the base of wooded hills, an artificial pond in the shape of a half-moon had been constructed. On an islet in the middle, the fairies dance with their queen, singing a song to the music of a consort:

> *Elisa* is the fairest Queene
> That euer trod vpon this greene
>
> .   .   .   .
>
> O blessed bee each day and houre,
> Where sweete *Elisa* builds her bowre.

The queen of the fairies, with a garland as an imperial crown, recites in blank verse:

> I that abide in places under-ground
> Aureola, the Queene of Fairy Land
>
> .   .   .   .
>
>   salute you with this chaplet,
> Giuen me by Auberon, the fairy King.

The Entertainment at Elvetham took place in the autumn of 1591, only a few years before even the latest possible date of *A Midsummer Night's Dream.* Even if Shakespeare had not attended it, this magnificent event was prepared by poets, artists, and musicians with whom he was acquainted. The quarto with the libretto, the lyrics, and the songs of the four-day spectacle in Elizabeth's honor, was published and twice reprinted. Oberon, Titania, and the fairies did not enter the Shakespearean comedy from old romances such as *Huon of Bordeaux,* but from the stage: perhaps from Greene's play *James IV* in which Oberon dances with the fairies and most certainly from Elizabethan masque and entertainment.

In masques and court pastorals, among the mythological figures next to Cupid we always find Mercury. In *A Midsummer Night's Dream* it appears that the place usually assigned to Mercury is empty. But Mercury is not merely the messenger, the *psychopompos* who induces and interrupts sleep as Puck and Ariel do. Hermes-Mercury belongs to the family of tricksters. The trickster is the most invariable, universal, and constant mythic character in the folklore of all peoples. As a mediator between gods and men—the bottom and the top—the trickster is a special broker: he both deceives the gods and cheats men. The trickster is the personification of mobility and changeability and transcends all boundaries, overthrowing all hierarchies. He turns everything upside-down. Within this world gone mad a new order emerges from chaos, and life's continuity is renewed.

> Jack shall have Jill,
> Nought shall go ill;
> The man shall have his mare again, and all shall be well.
>
> (3.2.461–63)

In the marvelous syncretism of *A Midsummer Night's Dream,* Puck the trickster is a bottom and carnivalesque translation of Cupid, Mercury, and Satyr. The Harlequin, Fool, and Lord of Misrule—called in Scotland the Abbot of Unreason—belong to this theatrical family of Tricksters. Puck's practical joke ("An ass's noll I fixed on his head" [3.2.17]) has its origin in the oldest tradition of folk festivities. Mummery, painting the face red or white, or putting grotesque or animal masques on the face, is still often seen during Twelfth Night, Ash Wednesday, or Valentine's Day.

But putting on an ass's head was not only a theatrical repetition of mockeries and jokes of the Feast of Fools or the day of Boy-Bishop. Another universal rite is also repeated when a "boore," a thing "base and vile," or a mock-king of the carnival was crowned, and after his short reign, uncrowned, thrashed, mocked, and abused. As the drunk Christopher Sly, a tinker, is led into the palace in *The Taming of the Shrew,* so the bully Bottom is introduced to Titania's court of fairies. A coronet of flowers winds through his hairy temples as a crown and the queen's servants fulfill all his fancies. Among Bottom's colleagues is also another "Athenian" tinker, Tom Snout. Like Christopher Sly and all mock-kings abused and uncrowned, Bottom wakes from his dream having played only the part of an ass.

The painting by Henry Fuseli, who was one of the most original illustrators of Shakespeare's plays, depicts Titania assuming the pose of Leonardo's *Leda.* She is nude, but her hair is carefully coiffed. She is calling upon her servants, but her eyes are half-closed as if in ecstasy. Next to Titania sits Bottom, hunched over. He appears sad or surprised. He is paying no attention to Titania or to Peaseblossom who is scratching his head. Titania's court—dwarfs, midgets, and ladies in waiting—is wearing Empire dresses. Bottom with his ass's head found himself at some court masque or feast whose sense he does not seem to grasp. Fuseli's painting dates from ca. 1780–1790.

Both in traditional performances of *A Midsummer Night's Dream*, in which Bottom's night at Titania's court is presented as a romantic ballet, and in the spectacle by Peter Brook and many of his followers emphasizing Titania's sexual fascination with a monstrous phallus (*mea culpa!*), the carnival ritual of Bottom's adventure was altogether lost. Even Lucius, as a frustrated ass in Apuleius, was amazed at the sexual eagerness of the Corinthian matron who, having "put off all her garments to her naked skinne . . . began to annoint all her body with balme" and caressed him more adeptly than "in the Courtsan schooles." Bottom appreciates being treated as a very important person, but is more interested in food than in the bodily charms of Titania.

In Bottom's metamorphosis and in his encounters with Titania, not only do high and low, metaphysics and physics, and poetry and farce meet, but so do two theatrical traditions: the masque and the court entertainment meet the carnival world turned upside-down. In masques and entertainments, "noble" characters were sometimes accompanied by Barbarians, Wild Men, Fishwives, and Marketwives. At the Entertainment at Elvetham an "ugly" Nereus showed up, frightening the court ladies. But for the first time in both the history of revels and the history of theater, Titania/Diana/the Queen of Fairies sleeps with a donkey in her "flowery bower." This encounter of Titania and Bottom, the ass and the mock-king of the carnival, is the very beginning of modern comedy and one of its glorious opening nights.

A musical interlude accompanies the transition from night to day in *A Midsummer Night's Dream:* "Winde Hornes, Enter Theseus, Egeus, Hippolita, and all his traine" (Stage Direction 4.1.101 Folio). In this poetic discourse, the blowing of the hunters' horns, the barking of the hounds, and the echo from the mountains are translated into a musical opposition in the Platonic tradition of "discord" and "concord." In this opposition between day and night, not the night but precisely the musical orchestration of daybreak is called discord by Theseus and by Hippolyta. For Theseus this discord marks "the musical confusion / Of hounds and echo in conjunction" (4.1.109–10). "I never heard," replies Hippolyta, "so musical a discord, such sweet thunder" (116–17). Only a few lines further, when Lysander and Demetrius kneel at Theseus' feet after the end of "night-rule," the "discord" of the night turns into the new "concord" of the day: "I know you two are rival enemies / How comes this gentle concord in the world" (4.1.142).

Both terms of the opposition, "concord" and "discord," are connected by Theseus when Philostrate, his master of the revels, hands him the brief of an interlude to be presented by the "Athenian" mechanicals:

> 'A tedious brief scene of young Pyramus
> And his love Thisbe; very tragical mirth.'?
> Merry and tragical? Tedious and brief?
> That is hot ice and wonderous strange snow!
> How shall we find the concord of this discord?
> (5.1.56–60)

This new *concordia discors* is a tragicomedy, and good Peter Quince gives a perfect definition of it when he tells the title of the play to his actors: "Marry, our play is 'The most lamentable comedy, and most cruel death of Pyramus and Thisbe' " (1.2.11–12). Although merely an Athenian carpenter, as it turns out, Quince is quite well-read in English repertory, having styled the title of his play after the "new tragical comedy" *Damon and Pithias* by Edwards (1565), or after Preston's *Cambises* (published ca. 1570), a "lamentable comedy mixed full of pleasant mirth." The same traditional titles, judged by printers to be attractive to readers and spectators, appeared on playbills and title pages of quartos: *The comicall History of the Merchant of Venice* or *The most Excellent and lamentable Tragedie of Romeo and Iuliet.* This last title would fit better the story of Pyramus and Thisbe.

We do not know and probably will not discover which of the plays, *Romeo and Juliet* or *A Midsummer Night's Dream,* was written earlier. History repeats itself twice, "the first time as tragedy, the second as farce." Marx was right: world history and the theater teach us that *opera buffa* repeats the protagonists and situations of *opera seria.* The "most cruel death" of Romeo and Juliet is changed into a comedy, but this comedy is "lamentable." The new tragicomedy, "concord of the discord," is a *double* translation of tragedy into a comedy and of comedy into burlesquing. The burlesque and the parody are not only in the dialogue and in the songs; the "lamentable comedy" is played at Theseus' wedding by the clowns.

Burlesque is first the acting and stage business. A wall separates the lovers, and they can only whisper and try to kiss through a "hole," a "cranny," or "chink." This scene's crudity is both naive and sordid, as in sophomoric jokes and jests where obscene senses are given to innocent words. Gestures here are more lewd than words.

The Wall was played by Snout. Bottom, who also meddled in directing, recommended: "Let him hold his fingers thus" (3.1.65–66).

But what was this gesture supposed to be? Neither the text nor stage directions ("Wall stretches out his fingers" [Stage Direction 5.1.175]) are clear. In the nineteenth-century tradition, the Wall stretched out his fingers while the lovers kissed through the "cranny." In Peter Hall's Royal Shakespeare Company film (1969), the Wall holds in his hands a brick which he puts between his legs. Only then does he make a "cranny" with his thumb and index finger. But it could have been yet another gesture. The "hole," as the letter *V* made by the middle and index finger, would be horizontal and vertical. As Thomas Clayton argues, Snout in the Elizabethan theater of clowns straddled and stretched out his fingers between his legs wide apart. "And this the cranny is, right and sinister" (5.1.162). Snout, although an "Athenian" tinker, had a taste of Latin or Italian and knew what "sinister" meant.

Romeo could not even touch Juliet when she leaned out the window. The Wall scene ("O kiss me through the hole of this vile wall" [198]) is the "bottom translation" of the balcony scene from *Romeo and Juliet*. The sequel of suicides is the same in both plays. But Thisbe "dies" differently. The burlesque Juliet on stage stabs herself perforce with the scabbard of Pyramus' sword. This is all we know for certain about how *A Midsummer Night's Dream* was performed in Shakespeare's lifetime.

The lovers from Athens did not meet a lion during their nightly adventure as Pyramus and Thisbe did in their forest, nor a dangerous lioness as Oliver and Orlando did in the very similar Arden forest of *As You Like It*. But the menace of death hovers over the couple from the very beginning: "Either to die the death, or to abjure" (1.1.65). The *furor* of love always calls forth death as its only equal partner. Hermia says to Lysander: "Either death or you I'll find immediately" (2.2.155); Lysander says of Helena: "Whom I do love, and will do till my death" (3.2.167); Helena says of Demetrius: "To die upon the hand I love so well" (2.1.244), and again: "'tis partly my own fault, / Which death, or absence soon shall remedy" (3.2.243–44). Even sleep "with leaden legs and batty wings" is "death counterfeiting" (3.2.364).

In these four voices of love frenzy, neither the classical Cupid with his "fiery shaft" nor the Neoplatonic Cupid with his "incorporeal eye" are present any longer. Desire ceases to use a paradigmatic language. Now desire is the action of the body: the hand which grabs for another hand to throw someone to the ground or to kill. The words "death" and "dead" are uttered twenty-eight times; "dying" and "die" occur fourteen times. Altogether, the linguistic field of "death" appears in nearly fifty verses of *A Midsummer Night's Dream* and is distributed almost evenly among the events in the forest and the play at Theseus's wedding.

The frequency of "kill" and "killing" is thirteen, and "sick" and "sickness" occur six times. In *A Midsummer Night's Dream*, which has often been called a happy comedy of love, "kiss" and "kissing" occur only six times, always within the context of the burlesque; "joy" occurs eight times, "happy" six, and "happiness" none.

The forest happenings during the premarital night are only the first revels and sports in *A Midsummer Night's Dream*; the main merriment is provided by clowns. In the "mirths," in the forest and at court, Bottom is the leading actor. While rehearsing his part in the forest, "sweet Pyramus" was "translated" into an ass. He "dies" on stage as Pyramus, only to be called an ass by Theseus: "With the help of a surgeon, he might yet recover, and prove an ass" (5.1.298–300).

If Bottom's metamorphoses in the forest and at court are read synchronically, as one reads a musical score, the "sweet bully" boy in both of his roles—as an ass and as Pyramus—sleeps with the queen of the fairies, is crowned and uncrowned, dies, and is resurrected on stage. The true director of the night-rule in the woods is Puck, the Lord of Misrule. The interlude of Pyramus and Thisbe was chosen for the wedding ceremonies by Philostrate, the master of revels to Theseus. Within *A Midsummer Night's Dream*, performed as an interlude at an aristocratic wedding, the play within a play is a paradigm of comedy as a whole. *A Midsummer Night's Dream* has an enveloping structure: the small "box" repeats the larger one, as a Russian doll contains smaller ones.

The brutal and violent change of desire during a single night and the pre-wedding night with a "monster" do not appear to be the most appropriate themes for wedding entertainment. Neither is the burlesque suicide of the antique models of Romeo and Juliet the most appropriate merriment for "a feast in great solemnity." All dignity and seriousness is absent from the presentation of "most cruel death of Pyramus and Thisbe." The night adventures of Titania and two young couples is finally nullified and reduced to a "dream."

"The lunatic, the lover and the poet, / Are of imagination all compact" (5.1.7–8). These lines of Theseus, like those of Helena's monologue from the first scene in act 1, are a part of the poetic metadiscourse whose theme is self-referent: the dreams in *A Midsummer Night's Dream* and the whole play. And as in Helena's soliloquy, Neoplatonic oppositions return in it.

Ficino, in *In Platonis Phaedrum* and in *De amore,* distinguishes four forms of inspired madness—*furor divinus:* the "fine frenzy" of the poet; "the ravishment of the diviner"; "the prophetic rapture of the mystic"; and the "ecstasy of the lover"—*furor amatorius.*

Even more important than the repetition of Neoplatonic categories of "madness" is the inversion by Theseus/Shakespeare of the values and hierarchy in this exchange of signs:

> The poet's eye, in a fine frenzy rolling,
> Doth glance from heaven to earth, from earth to heaven;
> And as imagination bodies forth
> The forms of things unknown, the poet's pen
> Turns them to shapes, and gives to airy nothing
> A local habitation and a name.
>
> (5.1.12–17)

As opposed to the "fine frenzy" of the Platonic poet, Shakespeare's pen gives earthly names to shadows, "airy nothing," and relocates them on earth. The "lunatic" who "sees more devil than vast hell can hold" (5.1.9) replaces Neoplatonic mystics. The frenzied lover "sees Helen's beauty in a brow of Egypt" (5.1.11). All three—"the lunatic, the lover, and the poet"—are similar to a Don Quixote who also gave in to phantasies, shadows of wandering knights, the "local habitation and a name"; who saw beautiful Dulcinea in an ugly country maid; and, like a Shakespearean madman who in a "bush supposed a bear" (5.1.22) would charge windmills with his lance, taking them to be wizards, and stormed wineskins, thinking them to be brigands.

> Lovers and madmen have such seething brigands,
> Such shaping phantasies, that apprehend
> More than cool reason ever comprehends.
>
> (5.1.4–6)

In this metadiscourse, which is at the same time self-defeating and self-defending, a manifesto of Shakespeare's dramatic art and a defense of his comedy are contained. "More than cool reason ever comprehends" is not the Platonic "shadow" and the metaphysical *supra intellectum* of Pico and Ficino. "More than cool reason ever comprehends" is, as in Paul, the "foolish things of the world" which God designed "to confound the wise." This "foolishness of God," taken from the Corinthians, read and repeated after the carnival tradition, is the defense of the Fool and the praise of Folly.

The lunatics—the Fool, the Lord of Misrule, the Abbott of Unreason—know well that when a true king, as well as the carnival mock-king, is thrown off, he is turned into a thing "base and vile, holding no quantity"; that on Earth there are "more devils than vast hell can hold" and that Dianas, Psyches, and Titanias sleep not with winged Cupids but with asses; but what is this Bacchic ass of Saturnalia and carnival? "Bless thee, Bottom, bless thee! Thou art translated" (3.2.113). The Bottom translation is the wisdom and the language of the Fool.

Exchanging Visions: Reading
A Midsummer Night's Dream

David Marshall

"Spirits and fairies cannot be represented, they cannot even be painted,
—they can only be believed." *A Midsummer Night's Dream* seems
designed to engage the issue at stake in this assertion of Charles Lamb's.
Lamb makes his claim after drawing the conclusion that "the plays of
Shakespeare are less calculated for performance on a stage, than those
of almost any other dramatist whatever." Although he is writing about
the fitness of Shakespeare's tragedies for stage representation, one often
has the sense that he is describing the problems presented by producing
Shakespeare's "dream play." As spectators to stage representations,
writes Lamb, "we find to our cost that instead of realizing an idea, we
have materialized and brought down a fine vision to the standard of
flesh and blood. We have to let go a dream. . . ." Five years after the
publication of Lamb's essay, in 1816, William Hazlitt took Lamb's
position; while watching a performance of *A Midsummer Night's Dream,*
Hazlitt realized that the play could not be represented on the stage. His
review for the *Examiner* begins: "We hope we have not been accessory
to murder, in recommending a delightful poem to be converted into a
dull pantomime. . . . We have found to our cost, once for all, that the
regions of fancy and the boards of Covent Garden are not the same
thing. All that was fine in the play, was lost in the representation."
Hazlitt's rehearsal of this review in the pages of his *Characters of Shakespeare's Plays* shows that he was responding not to a particular performance but to what he saw as the character of the stage: "Poetry and

From *ELH* 49, no. 3 (Fall 1982). © 1982 by the Johns Hopkins University Press.

the stage do not agree well together. . . . The *idea* can have no place upon the stage, which is a picture without perspective; everything there is in the foreground. That which was merely an airy shape, a dream, a passing thought, immediately becomes an unmanageable reality. . . ." As a play of rare visions, airy shapes, and dreams, *A Midsummer Night's Dream* stages the dilemma of how to marry poetry to the stage.

Of course, Lamb and Hazlitt could be accused of reading Shakespeare from the standpoint of English Romanticism—of trying to turn public plays into private poems. Both are also reacting to the conventions of the nineteenth-century stage: what Lamb calls "contemptible machinery" and "the elaborate and anxious provision of scenery." Clearly, these are not the conditions of dramatic illusion that the prologue to *Henry V* figures in its invocation of the audience's powers of imagination. Their responses, however, should not be disregarded. Lamb and Hazlitt have realized that in the theater a vision of a play is expounded and imposed upon them. Each finds to his cost that some impression of his fantasy has been stolen. I will argue that the experiences of these specators—these points of view—begin to represent a reading of *A Midsummer Night's Dream*; they reflect the play's presentation and dramatization of the conditions of theater. Hazlitt, in particular, asks us to see that the question of the *Dream's* fitness for the stage is posed by the play itself; he frames a double simile: "Fancy cannot be embodied any more than a simile can be painted; and it is as idle to attempt it as to personate *Wall* or *Moonshine*." Hazlitt's allusion to the mistaken enterprise of the play within the play suggests that *A Midsummer Night's Dream* might contain a dangerous · acknowledgement: a threat that the representation of the play itself might be undone. By *undone* I mean not only the senses of incomplete, ruined, negated, and expounded, but also the sense in which the scene that Shakespeare refused to represent before the audience of *The Winter's Tale* is said to be undone by its mere narration: Shakespeare withholds from our sight an encounter which, we are told, "lames report to follow it and undoes description to do it." Hazlitt asserts that the attempt to present Shakespeare's *Dream* on the stage would be as counter-productive and literal minded as the mechanicals' attempt to figure moonshine; and he implies that the play within the play, in reflecting and figuring the problems of representing *A Midsummer Night's Dream*, might undo Shakespeare's impossible enterprise.

Hazlitt's perspective is an extreme manifestation of what was to become a commonplace in nineteenth-century Shakespeare criticism. ("It has often been remarked," wrote Maginn, "that it is impossible to play the enchanted scenes of Bottom to any effect.") But most critics have presumed that *A Midsummer Night's Dream* is in fact fit for stage representation. Dowden, for example, admits that the mechanicals "serve as an indirect apology for [Shakespeare's] own necessarily imperfect attempt to represent fairy land" but claims (with Gervinus) that the play's acknowledgment of the limitations of theatrical illusion really differentiates Shakespeare from inept attempts "to leave nothing to be supplied by the imagination." This has become the predominant point of view in the twentieth century: C. L. Barber attacks Hazlitt and declares, "Shakespeare, in *his* play, triumphantly accomplishes just this hard thing, 'to bring moonlight into a chamber.'" David P. Young agrees: "Where the mechanicals fail at dramatic illusion . . . *A Midsummer Night's Dream* succeeds." Perhaps the conventions of the modern stage—a physical and imaginative space which has been transformed by film, stylization, Brecht, and the magic of technology—have returned us to the sensibilities suggested in the prologue to *Henry V*. Today, representing Shakespeare's dramatic illusions on the stage doesn't strike us as a problem.

However, it may be that, enchanted with the play, we too easily assume that any comparison it makes between itself and the mechanicals' play is self-congratulatory. Lamb and Hazlitt's perhaps perverse or anachronistic points of view—their visions of *A Midsummer Night's Dream* and its problems—might teach us another way to look at Shakespeare's play. The point is not to take sides in the debate about whether the play can be represented but to recognize how seriously the play addresses and is addressed by the specter of moonshine. Let us return to the terms and the scene of Hazlitt's double simile: "Fancy cannot be embodied any more than a simile can be painted; and it is as idle to attempt it as to personate *Wall* or *Moonshine*." Readers and spectators have agreed that this moonshine can be seen as a figure for all that is shining, magical, and dream-like in *A Midsummer Night's Dream*, even if they have disagreed about how it reflects upon Shakespeare's enterprise of picturing on the stage a night-world of visions and imaginary characters. The mechanicals have been seen as placing both too much and too little faith in theatrical illusions (hence their fears about the audience's belief in lions and walls). Their comedy lies partly in their literalization of what should remain figured and figurative. But we need to see that this literalization becomes a figure for the dilemma of the play—a dilemma that Hazlitt figures in terms of figurative language. To embody fancy and to personate moonshine are like trying to paint a simile, to map out or spell out what cannot be pictured as such; and a figure cannot be figured in this sense without becoming literalized—or lost.

This predicament becomes more clear if we look at the language of Shakespeare's text at the famous moment when the mechanicals arrive at the proper prop to stand for moonshine. After Bottom suggests that real moonshine be allowed to play itself, Peter Quince replies: "Ay; or else one must come in with a bush of thorns and a lantern, and say he comes to disfigure, or to present, the person of Moonshine" (3.2.59–61). The verb *to disfigure* in this line is always glossed as a characteristic malapropism, a humorous mistake made by Quince as he means to say *to figure*; that is, *to represent*. But this verbal mistake, this moment of misspeaking, can be read as a "Freudian slip" on the part of the play's unconscious—or as a signal that the problem of the play may appear in a play of words. We must read Quince's line not just as an appropriate mistake but as something Shakespeare meant to say. What then, is the status of the *or* in the formulation "to disfigure, or to present"? Is Quince juxtaposing two alternate possibilities or is he using the terms synonymously? The possibility of representing the play resides in the answer to this question. For the threat of the mechanicals' literal-mindedness would be its reflection of the inevitable *disfiguring* inherent in presenting moonshine. Looking at Quince's terms from Hazlitt's perspective we see that *to present is to disfigure*. The question of the play is whether presenting and representing must mean misrepresenting; whether *figure* must be synonymous with *disfigure;* whether *figure* must mean or even might mean *literalize,* or literally, *de-figure.*

Hazlitt's and Lamb's views about the fitness of *A Midsummer Night's Dream* for stage representation may or may not be persuasive, but they can teach us that one way to see the play is to recognize in this comic moment a figure for the possibility of the play's impossibility. This would allow us to realize the senses in which the play is about problems of representation and figuration: not only whether the play can be staged but also what it means to present a vision or an image to someone else's mind, to ask another person to see with one's eyes, to become a spectator to someone else's vision. Such questions themselves raise questions about the conditions of theater: the power of one imagination over others; the power to enchant and transform vision;

the possibility of autonomous minds or imaginations sharing dreams and fantasies; the difference between picturing a text in private reading and attending a public, collective spectacle. *A Midsummer Night's Dream* asks us to take seriously the dilemma of joining poetry and the stage. In adopting this perspective we will find ourselves considering yet another question: the possibility of what Shakespeare elsewhere called "the marriage of true minds."

II

In the first part of *Die Wahlverwandtschaften,* the Count delivers a short lecture on comedies and marriage, as if he were a cynical Northrop Frye:

> The comedies which we see so often are misleading; they tempt our imagination away from the realities of the world. In a comedy we see marriage as an ultimate goal, reached only after surmounting obstacles which fill several acts; and at the moment when this goal is achieved, the curtain falls and a momentary satisfaction warms our hearts. But it is quite different in life. The play goes on behind the scenes, and, when the curtain rises again, we would rather not see or hear any more of it.

Goethe's novel is about points of view, perspectives, and spectacles. In it characters are reduced to interchangeable pairs of A,B,C, and D; lovers are substituted for one another by mysterious and altering affinities. I can imagine that *Elective Affinities* is in part a parodic translation of *A Midsummer Night's Dream,* and I introduce the Count's speech here to read it as an ironic commentary on Shakespeare's play. The Count's remarks make Charlotte "uneasy" and eventually "determined to stop this sort of talk once and for all"; but I hope they will remind us that plays that end in marriage are not necessarily comedies. In fact, *A Midsummer Night's Dream,* which raises the curtain on a parody of *Romeo and Juliet* after its marriages have been performed, seems to invite speculation about what will go on—and what has gone on—behind its scenes. Is it asking too much of an antique fable and a fairy toy to be skeptical about the "gentle concord" created by the sudden reconciliation and rearrangement of the lovers at the end of the play? How are we to take Demetrius' recovery from the "sickness" of abandoning Helena and loving Hermia since it is just as much the product of enchantment as Lysander's abandonment of Hermia and love for Helena? Are we to be pleased by the success of Helena's subjection of herself to Demetrius or Titania's sudden and manipulated surrender to Oberon? What about Hippolyta's marriage to the soldier who vanquished her? These are questions that are not presented by the traditional view of the play as a "wedding present" and an epithalamium in which there is a "festive confidence that things will go right." They raise the possibility that *A Midsummer Night's Dream* is not "one of Shakespeare's happiest comedies [as Madeleine Doran claims in her introduction to The Penguin edition]" but rather a "most lamentable comedy" (1.2.11–12) and "very tragical mirth" (5.1.57).

We don't need to imagine another act, however, to doubt the play's status as a happy comedy. Indeed, as the curtain rises on the first scene, despite some elegant poetry, we have no reason to believe that the conflicts unfolding before us will be resolved any more comically than those of, say, *The Winter's Tale* or even *King Lear*. Even before Hermia is threatened with death in order to force her to marry against her will, the stage is set with an exchange between Theseus and Hippolyta that could be played as tense rather than as festive. Hippolyta speaks only once in the first scene—and she doesn't speak again until the fourth act—yet critics have usually acted as if they knew what was going on in her mind. C. L. Barber describes the characters looking toward their wedding in this way: "Theseus looks forward to the hour with masculine impatience, Hippolyta with a woman's willingness to dream away the time." I don't know how Barber manages to assign genders to these feelings, but, more important, I fail to see any sign of either happiness or willingness in Hippolyta's response to Theseus' expression of impatience. Hippolyta speaks with dignity, reason, and diplomacy—as is appropriate for a queenly prisoner-of-war—but her words are restrained and noncommittal:

> Four days will quickly steep themselves in night,
> Four nights will quickly dream away the time;
> And then the moon, like to a silver bow
> New-bent in heaven, shall behold the night
> Of our solemnities.

> (1.1.7–11)

Theseus, in his opening speech, has figured the moon "Like to a stepdame or a dowager, / Long withering out a young man's revenue" (5–6), thereby inaugurating the play's pervasive imagery of gain and loss and prefiguring Lysander's plan to "steal" Hermia by fleeing to his "widow aunt, a dowager / Of great revenue" (1.1.156–57). Hippolyta's response pictures the moon as a "silver bow / New-bent": under this sign will an Amazon warrior marry the prince who admits to her, "I wooed thee with my sword, / And won thy love doing thee injuries" (16–17). Theseus' "nuptial hour" (1) becomes Hippolyta's "solemnities" (a term that will echo throughout the play, conveying a sense of gravity as well as ceremony). But the most telling interpretation of Hippolyta's revision of these figures comes from Theseus himself. He replies by telling Philostrate to "Stir up the Athenian youth to merriments, / Awake the pert and nimble spirit of mirth, / Turn melancholy forth to funerals; / The pale companion is not for our pomp" (12–15). Theseus addresses Philostrate but clearly he is responding to Hippolyta, as if she were playing Hamlet to his Claudius. He has heard and seen a mournful melancholy in his bride-to-be, not a happy willingness, and he reminds her that they are going to a wedding and not a funeral. Then he thinks to acknowledge that he has wooed her with his sword and done her injuries—one critic [W. Moelwyn Merchant] calls this a "ravishment disguised in [an] oblique courtesy"—but he assures her: "I will wed thee in another key, / With pomp, with triumph, and with revelling" (18–19). It has been argued [by David P. Young] that Theseus "prizes harmony," but how will the key of this wedding be different from the key in which he won Hippolyta's "love" (his word, not hers) in combat? Pomp, revelling, and particularly triumph sound as much like a military celebration as a wedding; and we should note the possibility of a textual pun produced by the orthography which rendered "revelling" as "reuelling"—which on the page "sounds" like "ruling." Characteristically, Hippolyta does not respond to this half-apologetic assertion of will; nor does she break her silence when Theseus turns to her and says, "Come, my Hippolyta. What cheer, my love?" (122) after he has faced Hermia with the choices of marrying according to her father's will, "death, or . . . a vow of single life" (121). What cheer, indeed, would Hippolyta express in response to this scene of wooing with a sword? It is hard to imagine her in the first scene as "a tamed and contented bride [as Celeste Turner Wright describes her]," particularly since Theseus seems to have trouble picturing her in this way.

Hippolyta stands as more than an ornament for a masque; her silence is an important key to the conflicts of *A Midsummer Night's Dream*. The problem of how to read her silence—and what it means to imagine what is going on behind the scenes, as it were, in the privacy of her mind—is one of the problems the play can teach us about. As readers who must imagine Hippolyta represented on a stage, we must first hear her silence; we must recognize that she does not speak. Traditionally, however, critics seem to have identified with Theseus at the beginning of the play. They have adopted his point of view, and, in imposing his sentiments upon his bride, they have read happiness in her silence, thus reenacting the telling mistake of Peter Quince in scene 2 when he speaks of playing before "the Duke and Duchess on *his* wedding day" (1.2.6–7, my emphasis). David P. Young, who dedicates a chapter about order to Theseus, agrees with other critics about the limits of Theseus' vision in act 5, but sees the first scene with Theseus' eyes: "It is appropriate that Theseus, as representative of daylight and right reason, should have subdued his bride-to-be to the rule of his masculine will. That is the natural order of things." This *may* have been the ruling ideology in the sixteenth century or in 1966—I don't see that it has ever been the *natural* order of things—but it is not necessarily the ideology of *A Midsummer Night's Dream.* We should be willing to consider Hippolyta's fortunes as the curtain rises, in the same way that she perhaps weeps Hermia's fortunes in the first scene; to do this, we must take her eyes.

Hippolyta is not silent for the reasons that Cordelia decides to "love, and be silent." Nor is she performing the "perfect ceremony of love's rite" in which one must "learn to read what silent love has writ." Hippolyta is, I believe, tongue-tied, as if she were the serious reflection of Bottom at the moment when Titania comically ravishes him with the command to her fairies: "Tie up my lover's tongue, bring him silently" (3.1.186). Theseus (who has "heard" of Demetrius' inconsistency but "being over-full of self-affairs" [1.1.111–13] manages at least twice to forget about it) can therefore hear in Hippolyta's silence what he likes. He describes himself meeting frightened subjects who, unable to speak,

> dumbly have broke off,
> Not paying me a welcome. Trust me, sweet,
> Out of this silence yet I picked a welcome,
> And in the modesty of fearful duty
> I read as much as from the rattling tongue
> Of saucy and audacious eloquence.
> Love, therefore, and tongue-tied simplicity
> In least speak most, to my capacity.
> (5.1.98–105)

These are noble sentiments; but if Hippolyta is tongue-tied (and she is silent after this speech as well), it does not necessarily follow that one should read love in her silence. Part of Theseus' judgment against Hermia's advocacy of her own will cites that she is "wanting [her] father's voice" (52); that is, she lacks her father's consent *and* she wants to speak in her father's voice, to speak with his authority. Theseus tells Hermia that her voice has no standing in his court; her appeal is overruled because her plea must fall on deaf ears. I suggest that both Hermia and Hippolyta are in effect tongue-tied in the same way: their fate is to have others dictate their sentiments while they are silent or silenced.

The dispute over Hermia is after all the real drama of the first act—to which the brief monologues of Theseus and Hippolyta stand as a prologue. This dispute is figured as an economic one: Egeus insists that his daughter is private property ("she is mine, and all my right of her / I do estate unto Demetrius" [97–98]) which Lysander is trying to "filch" (36). (We might imagine that Hermia is named after Hermes: the master thief, the god of commerce and the market place, and the god of dreams.) However, the struggle over Hermia is also pictured as a conflict over control of her imagination and vision. Egeus accuses Lysander: "thou hast given her rhymes . . . / Thou hast by moonlight at her window sung / With feigning voice verses of feigning love, / And stol'n the impression of her fantasy . . ." (28–32). This is not the same accusation as when Hermia calls Helena a "thief of love" who has "stol'n my love's heart from him" (3.2.283–84). Egeus is complaining that Lysander with his voice and poems and fictions and trinkets of love has inscribed his own figure upon Hermia: in the paraphrase of one editor [Madeleine Doran], "stealthily imprinted thine image upon her fancy." This is a kind of theft because the act of imposing or imprinting upon her imagination, as Theseus figures it, belongs to Egeus. *Her* impression is seen as rightfully *his,* which is why Hermia's claim to think and speak for herself is also a crime against her father. Theseus pictures the situation for Hermia in this manner:

> To you your father should be as a god,
> One that composed your beauties; yea, and one
> To whom you are but as a form in wax,
> By him imprinted, and within his power
> To leave the figure, or disfigure it.
>
> (47–51)

Hermia, in Theseus' eyes, first seems her father's creation: a mixture of Eve and Galatea; but then in Theseus' revision of his figure (which makes more omnious his reference to his wedding with Hippolyta as "the sealing day betwixt my love and me" [84]), Hermia becomes a character stamped upon blank wax. It is her father's right to impress his own image upon this wax, to imprint a figure or disfigure it, to dictate what she represents and what she represents to herself: how she looks. "I would my father looked but with my eyes" (56), complains Hermia. Theseus insists: "Rather your eyes must with his judgment look" (57). Hermia is told to "choose love by another's eyes" (140), to see what others have figured for her fantasy—just as Hippolyta is asked (or assumed) to see her wedding from Theseus' point of view.

This struggle over vision and imagination also characterizes the dispute between Oberon and Titania. Oberon's response to Titania's denial of his question, "Am I not thy lord?" (2.1.63) is to seek control over her sight, to steal the impression of her fantasy. His strategy and revenge is to "streak her eyes / And make her full of hateful fantasies" (2.1.257–58). With his magic he dictates how she will look and love, enthralling her eyes to Bottom's deformed shape until the moment he decides to "undo / This hateful imperfection of her eyes" (4.1.61–62) and let her "See as thou wast wont to see" (71). The changeling boy is ostensibly the object of contention between Oberon and Titania, an occasion for both jealousy and disobedience. But it also represents an impression of Titania's fantasy that has been stolen from Oberon; when he says, "I'll make her render up her page to me" (2.1.185), we can hear a play on words which resonates in the context of the images and figures we have been juxtaposing. Just as Egeus insists on imprinting his own figures upon Hermia, Oberon wants to be the author of Titania's page. Egeus says that Hermia is his to "render" (1.1.96); Oberon is determined to make Titania render up the blank page of her imagination, surrender the rival image impressed on her fancy. It is within his power to replace the image of her love with the disfigured head of Bottom, to command her sight and fancy, to "leave the figure, or disfigure it." As a god, by the authority of his magic, Oberon enacts literally what Egeus and Theseus can perform only figuratively (or by coercion) when they tell Hermia to "fit your fancies to your father's will" (1.1.118).

The cost of fitting one's fancy to someone else's will (or vision or representation) is the issue with which I began this account of *A Midsummer Night's Dream*. This issue returns us to the scene of the playhouse; but in the terms of Lamb and Hazlitt, we are speaking of what was from the outset the price of admission to the theater. As we become spectators to a representation of the play, we must exchange our privately imagined readings for a publicly shared spectacle and allow ourselves to be silenced and impressed by someone else's vision and point of view. It is fitting, then, that the play should raise its curtain on the imposition of a point of view on tongue-tied Hippolyta, the stealing of Hermia's fantasy and the imprinting of a character on her imagination, and the transformation of Titania into a blank page to be written and figured upon by someone else's fancy. *A Midsummer Night's Dream* presents a political question: whether these women will be authors of their own characters or representations upon which the voices and visions of others will be dictated and imprinted. The dramatization of this situation, however, simultaneously presents us with a figure for the conditions of theater.

This double vision is focused by the parallel formulations which we have seen as figuring what is at stake in each of these situations: the mechanicals' scheme "to disfigure, or to present, the person of Moonshine" and Theseus' view of Hermia as a "form in wax" which her father has "imprinted" with the "power / To leave the figure or disfigure it." We remarked that Quince's supposed malapropism raised the possibility that to present or figure moonshine (the figure of *A Midsummer Night's Dream*) might mean to disfigure it. We took seriously the way that Quince's formulation may mean its "or" to join synonyms rather than separate alternatives. Obviously, Theseus in his phrase doesn't *mean* to appose the acts of figuring and disfiguring as synonyms; but how stable is the "or" which stands between imprinting a figure and disfiguring? The parallel situations of Hermia, Hippolyta, and Titania should make us wonder how the figuring and imprinting pictured by Theseus would be *different* from disfiguring. From Egeus' capacity to claim Hermia as his own printed character—and his reading of that character's autonomy as the imprint of another man—to Oberon's more literal (if not more real) tyranny over Titania's vision and imagination, the play shows impressing a figure and point of view upon someone else's imagination as disfiguring. These terms, then, reflect and are reflected by the dilemma of staging the play, which is also the dilemma of watching the play represented, as well as the problem of reading and writing about the play. By making these claims I do not mean to neutralize the political conflicts of *A Midsummer Night's Dream* (here dramatized in terms of the domination of women) by translating them into problems of representation. Rather, I hope to show that the realm of politics and the realm of poetry and theater here should be seen to figure each other. As spectators to these scenes we must acknowledge our roles as men and women *and* our roles as actors and spectators in a theater. This, too, is the price of admission.

III

Reading *A Midsummer Night's Dream* in the lights I am proposing makes it difficult to imagine that even with its comic scenes the play would have made a very suitable wedding present. (This is assuming, of course, that the play or some version resembling the text of the First Quarto was indeed performed at a wedding—something we do not know.) It often seems as appropriate as the play that Philostrate describes to Theseus as "against your nuptial" (5.1.75); and just as the prologue to that play excuses, "If we offend, it is with our good will" (5.1.108), Puck's epilogue acknowledges the possibility that "we shadows have offended" (5.1.413). Lovers are not presented in a very sympathetic light, even if one allows them their follies. This is reflected in the question Bottom asks when, in the scene following the dispute over Hermia, he is assigned the part of Pyramus: "What is Pyramus? a lover or a tyrant?" (1.2.19). Bottom's pairing of these stock roles is perhaps a logical, if comic, question; but it offers yet another formulation in which the status of an "or" is ambiguous. For in Theseus, Demetrius, and Oberon (and indirectly in Egeus, who takes Demetrius' part) we see men who are lovers *and* tyrants. Again, we wonder if the play will show us a difference between these two choices. The tyranny of the two kings in response to women who would control their own vision might authorize one to read a textual pun or hear the echo of a psychological association between the phrases "If he come not, then the play is marr'd. It goes forward, doth it" (4.2.5–6) and the phrases ten lines later ". . . there is two or three lords and ladies more married. If our sport had gone forward . . ." (4.2.16–17). Whether one imagines an association between the two lines or not, the play suggests that getting *married* might mean getting *marr'd*, especially if we hear in *marr'd* its sense of "disfigured."

I should acknowledge again that the point of view I have been expounding goes against what seems to be the predominant assumption that *A Midsummer Night's Dream* is a play which makes "luminous a traditional understanding of marriage." I quote this phrase from an impressive and scholarly article that I will take to be representative of this assumption, Paul A. Olson's "*A Midsummer Night's Dream* and the Meaning of Court Marriage." Professor Olson sets out to present "a cursory survey of Renaissance thought concerning the function of festival drama and the significance of wedlock" and then reads *A Midsummer Night's Dream* in this context. He commands an array of sources to claim that marriage, for the Elizabethans, "maintained the patterned hierarchy of society" and "fulfilled its part in the concord of things when the male ruled his mate in the same way that reason was ordained to control both will and passions." However, when the article imposes this ideology, and its twentieth century legacy, upon the play, I want to object on two related grounds. First, we should understand both the uses and the limits of entirely circumstantial evidence. Information about historical and intellectual context can help us to locate where the play takes place and what ideologies it must depend upon or resist as it stakes out a position. However, with such an understanding we may discover in the play a scene of struggle— either a reflection of, or an engagement in, struggle—and not necessarily a display of power: a representation of power relations which confirms or reinforces a particular world-view. This leads to my second point: in considering *A Midsummer Night's Dream*, the recognition of traditional views or relations should not be substituted for a reading of the conflicts that are acted out in the play.

To claim [as Olson does], for example, that "the movement toward an orderly subordination of the female and her passions to the more reasonable male" is "epitomized" in the marriage of Theseus and Hippolyta is to turn one's eyes from the contrast, as the play begins, between Theseus' impatience for his wedding night and Hippolyta's reasoned patience. It is also to be as forgetful as Theseus is of Demetrius' seemingly unreasonable and (dare I say) wanton conduct. Simply to assume [as Olson does] that Shakespeare adopted conventional models of Theseus as "the reasonable man and the ideal ruler" and Hippolyta as the Amazon who stood for "a false usurpation of the duties of the male reason by the lower female passions" is to insure that the conflicts of the first act—Hippolyta's silence and Hermia's desire to speak with her father's (that is, her own) voice—will fall on deaf ears. Olson quotes from Celeste Turner Wright's survey of "The Amazons in English Literature" but ignores her too brief speculation on risks and possibilities involved in portraying an Amazon on the English stage while Elizabeth played the role of Virgin Queen. Furthermore, who is

Theseus, that he should overrule Kent's lessons about blind respect for the authority of kings? There is more to take issue with: Oberon is assumed to be justified in seeking sovereignty over Titania, who becomes a representative of "the forces of the lower passions in man" and "princess of sensual passion." Oberon's behavior is ignored as male critics indulge their fantasies about Titania's supposedly "erotic games with Bottom and the changeling." However, my aim here is not so much to refute Olson's position as to suggest what it must ignore and, more important, to propose that the terms and context that Olson construes may indeed be present in the play, but not as a representation of the "Renaissance concept" of marriage (a concept too easily assumed to be stable, known, and even "natural").

Suppose that we opted not to see the play and its marriages through the eyes of Theseus. Critics have recognized that the famous fifth act monologue in which Theseus opposes reason and the imagination serves to mark the limits of his rationality. I think that the struggles between men and women in *A Midsummer Night's Dream* also place his embodiment of order, reason, and power in an ironic light. One way to picture this (in addition to the readings I have proposed) would be to imagine Theseus as a relative, as it were, of another Greek tyrant: Pentheus in the story of the Bacchae. (Scholars tell us that Shakespeare did not read Euripides, whose works were a standard part of school curricula in Greek but were not translated. Shakespeare would have known the story of the Bacchae, however, at the very least from book 3 of Ovid's *Metamorphoses*.) Imagine a play in which a tyrant takes it on himself to defend male order and hierarchy against female rebellion and sexual frenzy, in part by seeking to imprison the women of his city. Suppose this ruler stands as a symbol of rationality, that his will to reason tries to explain away the irrational, that he denies the possibility of a collective hallucination. In this world the gods are not exempt from human passions; one god transforms and distorts the vision of a woman so that she takes a man's head for an animal's—or an animal's head for a man's. People wake from dreams and find everything seeming double. Is this the frenzy of Dionysus or a midsummer night's dream?

My purpose in proposing this double vision is to suggest that *A Midsummer Night's Dream* might parody and transform some elements of the Bacchae myth. To consider that story as an almost hidden model for Shakespeare's play would be one way to allow that if one *were* to read *A Midsummer Night's Dream* as a conflict between "masculine" principles of rationality and order and "female" principles of sexuality and passion, it would not necessarily follow that one should privilege these terms according to the values of traditional Christian hierarchies. The story of the Bacchae provides a model in which these values are reversed. It reflects an image of the limits of Theseus' imagination and vision as he (like Oberon) tries to repress "female" passion with "male" reason. At the least, we are reminded of a dialectic in which the poles are less than stable and alternative visions of the world are set in struggle. Furthermore, we should note that in Ovid's text the story of Pyramus and Thisby is told by a weaver as a story within the story of the Bacchae; just as, of course, the play of *Pyramus and Thisby* is presented by a weaver (and company) as a play within the play of *A Midsummer Night's Dream*.

IV

My quarrel with those who would see *A Midsummer Night's Dream* as a traditional celebration of marriage is not simply that they refuse to read parts of the play closely; it is that they act as if it were clear what marriage means to the play. I am claiming that the play swerves away from festive comedy as it radically places in question a social institution that embodies relations of power and stages conflicts of imagination, voice, and vision. However, to say that *A Midsummer Night's Dream* is "anti-marriage" also would be to stop short of understanding the different senses of marriage that the play is concerned with. On more than one level it mediates on the terms of marriage by considering the conditions of being sundered and being joined. From the outset we see lovers who want to be joined but who find themselves sundered: Demetrius has parted from Helena, Hermia and Lysander are threatened with separation and then divided; in addition, Oberon and Titania are divided because Titania will not part with the changeling boy. The situations which separate, divide, part, and mismatch these various pairs provide the comedy of errors of the middle acts. Then, after the supposedly "gentle concord" which occasions Theseus to command that the "couples shall eternally be knit" (4.1.184), we become spectators to the comic and tragic sundering of Pyramus and Thisby: questionable entertainment for a questionable wedding feast.

However, even if we want to believe that these marriages end the play happily, we must admit that all that has been sundered has not been joined. In particular, there remains the problem of Helena. Helena is a problem, to begin with, because she often seems to embody the opposites of the qualities shared by the other women in the play: defiance, self-respect, independence, dignity. Could it be to emphasize by contrast the paths that Hippolyta, Titania, and Hermia have not taken that Helena is made to tell Demetrius: "I am your spaniel; . . . The more you beat me, I will fawn on you . . . spurn me, strike me, / Neglect me, lose me. . . ." (2.1.203–6)? One way to understand this love would be to suppose that it is not love at all, or at least not love for Demetrius, or desire for his love. The speech I have just quoted from is a response to Demetrius' question: "do I not in the plainest truth / Tell you I do not nor cannot love you?" (2.1.200–1). Before begging that she be treated "as you use your dog" (210), Helena answers: "And even for that do I love you the more" (202). Is Helena's pursuit of Demetrius founded in an expectation that he will not love her? When Demetrius suddenly appears to love her after being transformed by Oberon's magic, she refuses to take his declarations seriously, to accept his claim of love. Indeed, her strategy to win "thanks" by the "dear expense" (1.1.249) of informing on Hermia and Lysander could hardly be designed to better her position in regard to Demetrius. Whereas their flight might have left Helena as a logical alternative for Demetrius to fall back upon—both Hermia and Lysander wish her luck wth this as they say goodbye—Helena's betrayal can serve only to prevent the union (and escape) of her two friends.

Suppose, however, that it is Hermia and not Demetrius that Helena hopes to catch. Recall the love poem contained in the expression of jealousy that Helena speaks to Hermia as her first lines in the play:

> Your eyes are lodestars, and your tongue's sweet air
> More tuneable to lark than to shepherd's ear
> When wheat is green, when hawthorn buds appear.
> Sickness is catching. O, were favor so,
> Yours would I catch, fair Hermia, ere I go;
> My ear should catch your voice, my eye your eye,
> My tongue should catch your tongue's sweet melody.
>
> (1.1.183–89)

Helena's declaration, with increasingly ambiguous possessives, moves away from a conceit about wanting to attract Demetrius. She would catch Hermia's favor, too; and, in another sense, she has caught this favor, like the "sickness" that Demetrius describes as his love for

Hermia. From Helena's point of view, stopping Hermia and Lysander would not necessarily result in the marriage of Hermia and Demetrius. By law Hermia has three choices and rather than marry Demetrius or die she may choose "a vow of single life" (1.1.121). Theseus describes this "maiden pilgrimage" (1.1.75) as the life of a "barren sister" (72), insisting "But earthlier happy is the rose distilled / Than that which, withering on the virgin thorn, / Grows, lives, and dies in single bless-edness" (76–78). Hermia vows, "So will I grow, so live, so die, my lord, / Ere I will yield my virgin patent up / Unto his lordship whose unwished yoke / My soul consents not to give sovereignty" (79–82). These choices and characterizations should be kept in mind because, for Helena, Hermia's "sister's vows" (3.2.199) are precisely what is at stake. They are what has been lost and what might be gained.

When Helena rejects Lysander's "vow" (3.2.124) of love, she declares in response to his oath: "These vows are Hermia's" (3.2.130). She means they are meant for Hermia, they belong to Hermia; but also, these are Hermia's vows, these are the vows that Hermia made, I recognize them. Lysander has just spoken of his "badge of faith" (127), figuring his tears as an identifyng family crest. A few moments later, Hermia appears on the scene and Helena bitterly reproaches her for forgetting the "sister's vows" (199) they shared, comparing their for-mer union to "coats in heraldry . . . crowned with one crest" (213–14). Weaving a complex fabric of images, Helena figures the past state of "childhood innocence" (202) which characterized their shared vows:

> We, Hermia, like two artificial gods,
> Have with our needles created both one flower,
> Both on one sampler, sitting on one cushion,
> Both warbling of one song, both in one key;
> As if our hands, our sides, voices and minds
> Had been incorporate. So we grew together,
> Like to a double cherry, seeming parted,
> But yet an union in partition—
> Two lovely berries moulded on one stem
>
> (203–11)

We can see this densely poetic emblem of female sexuality as a revision of Theseus's figuring of the maiden vow of single life: his "barren," "fruitless," state, his flower "withering on the virgin thorn" are trans-formed into a persuasive picture of "single blessedness" in which two "grow" as one, flowering and fruitful. "So will I grow," vows Hermia to Theseus; so did we grow, insists Helena with her vision of what is "maidenly" (217), with her picture of the "virgin patent" Hermia must exchange to "join with men" (216).

Hermia responds to Helena's long and intense monologue: "I am amazed at your passionate words" (220). She is amazed, I take it, both at Helena's paranoid assumption that there is a conspiracy to perscute her and at the passionate expression of her love; the latter passion forms and informs the bulk of Helena's speech. Hermia has allowed that "Before the time I did Lysander see, / Seemed Athens as a paradise to me" (1.1.204–5); but as she and Lysander prepare to "turn away [their] eyes" from Athens (218) and enter exile, she barely looks back at the "playfellow" (220) with whom she acted Adam and Eve in a garden of "childhood innocence . . . like two artificial gods." Helena, in contrast, surprises Hermia by describing this paradise with the pain of loss and the joy of recollection. What she describes is a kind of marriage, and we can hear her words echo as a version and inversion of the Church of England's wedding ceremony. Dwelling on the word "one," Helena declares herself to have been joined with Hermia as "one," "incorporate." (Her "We, Hermia . . ." sounds almost like a "royal we" rather than a first-person plural and direct address—as if the one name named them both.) She reproaches: "will you rent our ancient love asunder, / To join with men in scorning your poor friend?" (3.2.215–16). The wedding ceremony from the 1549 *Book of Common Prayer* states "that it should never be lawful to put asunder those whome [God] by matrimonie haddeste made one"; or, to quote its better known declaration: "Those whome God hath joyned together: let no man put asunder." Helena's appeal reworks these terms; she "chides" (218) Hermia for having sundered their union by joining with men—just as formerly they "chid the hasty-footed time / For parting us" (200–201).

The sense of Helena's characterization of their vows as the vows of marriage is underlined by a speech of Lysander's which strongly prefigures Helena's language and imagery. When Hermia and Lysander meet at the prearranged place in the woods where Hermia and Helena "Upon faint primrose beds were wont to lie, / Emptying our bosoms of their counsel sweet" (1.1.215–16), Lysander declares: "One turf shall serve as pillow for us both, / One heart, one bed, two bosoms, and one troth" (2.2.41–42). Already these lines, spoken on the "beds" that Helena and Hermia used to lie on, anticipate the imagery that Helena will use when she describes the same scene. Lysander continues:

> O, take the sense, sweet of my innocence.
> Love takes the meaning in love's conference.
> I mean that my heart unto yours is knit,
> So that but one heart can make of it;
> Two bosoms interchained with an oath—
> So then two bosoms and a single troth.
>
> (2.2.45–50)

We can read Lysander's oath as a double paraphrase: it takes the language of the wedding ceremony (which also speaks of God "knitting" the couple together and calls for each of the betrothed to "plight" to the other his or her "troth") and practically constitutes an official vow of marriage, and it doubles the figures Helena will speak—from the "cushion" to the single, incorporate body that two people seem to share. Helena's recital of the scene of her vows with Hermia is thereby turned into an echo of Lysander's secret ceremony, although the spectator learns retrospectively that Lysander is echoing the sister's vows. These juxtapositions of speeches and texts further identify the sundering Helena laments with the breaking of the vows of marriage: vows which (imagined or not) she appears to take much more seriously than those which Demetrius has broken.

Helena's monologue is one indication that sundering and joining appear as more than comic devices in *A Midsummer Night's Dream*. Her speech acts like a meditation on joining: moving from an association of words which are prefixed by *con* ("confederacy . . . conjoined . . . conspired . . . contrived . . .") to the stunning series of figures which culminate in the "double cherry, seeming parted, / But yet an union in partition" (3.2.209–10). We can further measure the seriousness of these images, as well as what they say about the conditions in which we find the play's characters, if we recognize in Helena's portrayal of an "ancient love" (3.2.215) and subsequent state of loss a picture of the emblem and story of love which Plato has Aristophanes present in *The Symposium*. Aristophanes' myth (which was extensively summarized in Ficino's popular commentary on *The Symposium*) proposes that we live in a fallen state, each of us a half of an original whole person from which we have been severed. Love, then, both heterosexual and homosexual, "restores us to our ancient state by attempting to weld two beings into one . . . this is what everybody wants, and everybody would regard it as the precise expression of this desire . . . that he should melt into his beloved, and that henceforth they should be one instead of two." Helena's vision of her lost union with Hermia, "As if our hands, our sides, voices, and minds / Had been incorporate" (3.2.207–8), evokes both this mythical, original condition and the restoration that love means in its sense of mending what has been sundered. Here Christian, classical, and mythic imagery seem to come together to figure Helena's perception that what had been joined together in her ancient love has been put asunder. These terms imply that Helena will be left apart, parted, denied the marriage in which she felt united, unless we are willing to see her enchanted reunion with Demetrius as a fitting compensation. In that case we could read Helena's last expression of sentiment in the play as the completion envisioned in the myth from *The Symposium:* "I have found Demetrius like a jewel, / Mine own and not mine own" (4.1.190–91). Helena has just agreed with Hermia that "everything seems double" (189) and she perhaps regards newly affectionate Demetrius with a look of dazed recognition, as if he were both familiar and strange, both a part of herself and not herself. (This might authorize the possibility proposed in *Variorum* [A New] / [Edition of Shakespeare] that "jewel" should read "gemell"—that is, twin.) However, in light of the context of this marriage—both the events leading up to it and the utter silence of Helena and Hermia throughout the last act—it is hard to imagine that such a union would adequately repair what has been sundered or restore what has been lost.

V

It makes sense to recall at this point that all of the mechanicals are concerned with some form or manner of joining. Carpenter, joiner, weaver, bellows mender, tinker, tailor; their occupations enact the preoccupations of *A Midsummer Night's Dream.* Two construct or put together, two mend and repair, one weaves and one sews. All join together what is apart or mend what has been rent, broken, or sundered. It is appropriate, then, that after Peter Quince assigns the roles of his play, he instructs the mechanicals: "But masters, here are your parts; and I am to entreat you, request you, and desire you to con them by tomorrow night" (1.2.88–90). The newly appointed players are told to con their parts, which we know means to learn their roles by heart; but in juxtaposition with "parts" we might also read *con* as the prefix that Helena mediates on in her monologue about sundering and joining—the letters that add the sense of "something joined together" to a word. For a moment vocation and avocation appear to coincide as these men who join and mend together are called upon to "con" their parts.

To be an actor, however, is to play a part, to create it, to become it on stage. To be an actor is to double and divide oneself, to discover oneself in two parts: both oneself and not oneself, both the part and not the part. The mechanicals feel compelled to acknowledge this on their stage: "tell them that I Pyramus am not Pyramus" (3.1.19), says Bottom the weaver; and so Snout the tinker declares himself Snout and a wall, and the lion insists that he is the lion and Snug the joiner, as if Brecht and not Peter Quince had produced this play. This is the world of the theater but its conditions also characterize the world of *A Midsummer Night's Dream*. There Hermia asks, "Am I not Hermia? Are you not Lysander?"(3.2.273) upon finding herself divided from her partner and replaced by someone else who had been assigned to her role. We have remarked that in the mirror image of this moment Helena calls Demetrius (her twin or not) "mine own and not mine own." It is with these double visions in mind that I want to imagine that scene (in which the lovers awaken from their dream-filled slumber) as an acknowledgment of the perpetual coming together of the world of the play and the world of the theater. Picture Demetrius saying, "These things seen small and undistinguishable / Like far-off mountains turned into clouds"; Hermia, too, beholds this vision— "Methinks I see these things with parted eye, / When everything seems double"—as does Helena: "So methinks; / And I have found Demetrius like a jewel, / Mine own, and not mine own" (4.1.186–91). What, however, are "these things"? The characters and events that they have woken up to, perhaps; or those that they have "dreamed." But imagine the actors speaking these lines in the direction of the audience, as if they were actors who had woken to find themselves on the playhouse stage. The effect would be similar to the moment of unconscious self-consciousness when, in another context, the audience watches Helena ask, "Then how can it be said I am alone / When all the world is here to look at me?" (2.1.225–26); or like the epilogue which Puck speaks to remind the audience that they have dreamed and slumbered in a theater. (In a sense, this exchange stands as the lovers' epilogue). Hermia's double vision of these things, her parted eye, comes from her parted I: the doubling and dividing of her "I" into two parts—Hermia and not Hermia, the part and the actor before us. This is the *dédoublement* that Diderot recognized as the actor's mode of being. Diderot also recognized that actors must see these things with parted eye because they must face the audience across an imaginary partition, an invisible wall, whether they pretend to speak across it or not. As actors they are kept apart, separated by the parts they play and the partitions they deliver across a distance. As spectators we must face the fact that they—and consequently we—are sundered.

Against this background, this theatrical representation of a world where people appear sundered from themselves and each other, we see the men who join things together try to con the parts of actors. Their play, "conned with cruel pain" (5.1.80), is of course about sundering: the story of two lovers who are parted first by their families and last by death—but most palpably by a wall. This wall is referred to in the prologue as the "vile Wall which did these lovers sunder" (5.1.80); and in language that also echoes and parodies key words from the lovers' speeches, Thisby apostrophizes:

> O Wall, full often hast thou heard my moans
> For parting my fair Pyramus and me.
> My cherry lips have often kissed thy stones,
> Thy stones with lime and hair knit up in thee.
>
> (5.1.186–89)

It has often been remarked that the play within the play reflects the comedy of errors that the lovers enacted in the woods, or the tragedy they might have produced; and that the newly married couples do not appear to notice this, although we might read their mixture of joking, interruption, silence, and impatience as an indication if not an acknowledgment of this recognition. However, we need to recognize as well the serious echoes that these terms and images of parting should recall by the fifth act: in particular, the ridiculous image of sundering that is presented and personated by one of the mechanicals. Separating the lovers but also providing a medium of communication, binding them in a union in partition, this wall stands both as a comic, literal-minded device *and* as a literalization of one of the play's key figures. The wall acts as a visual metaphor, a "translation of a metaphor in its literal sense" (to borrow Schlegel's description of Bottom's transmutation). The tragedy of Pyramus and Thisby that is told by Ovid's weaver is metamorphosed into a farce for the couples who, for better or for worse, have been "knit." However, at the center of this play within a play is a picture of what has been sundered: a partition that should also remind us of our place. Here is what has faced us throughout *A Midsummer Night's Dream*, what will face us still when we wake from the play and find ourselves in the theater.

These reflections should lead us to wonder about what we are laughing at when we find the mechanicals ridiculous. (This is where the play might be laughing at us.) What, after all, is more ridiculous: to personate the wall that stands between us, thereby insisting that we see it, or to act as if the wall is not there? We are told that the mistake of the mechanicals is to leave nothing to the spectators' imaginations, but *can* we be trusted to see the invisible walls that confront us? Are we so much more observant than the spectators to the play within the play? Throughout *A Midsummer Night's Dream* they figure beholders who can hardly see what is before them: each other or themselves. What is more ridiculous: to have someone "signify wall" or to "let him hold his fingers thus" (3.1.69)—as if either partitions or the people standing for them allowed us openings to see through; as if, like Lysander, we could wake from a death-like slumber and exclaim: "Transparent Helena, Nature shows art, / That through thy bosom makes me see thy heart" (2.2.104–5)? He is, of course, enchanted: dreaming. The theater presents itself as an imaginary "wooden O"(*Henry V*, 1.1.13) through or in which we may see its spectacles. But the theater must end by teaching us how to see—not only how to see through—the invisible wall that creates its architecture. This is a wall that we have to imagine to see, yet it won't disappear if we won't see it. Theater shows us both partitions and how we personate partitions. It allows us to hear "partitions discourse," to repeat the play on words Demetrius makes as he watches a man simultaneously present a text and a wall (5.1.165–66). This reminds us that texts, too, are walls that keep us asunder, although we might wish to deliver them, deliver ourselves from them, and thus present ourselves.

The theater sunders us and shows us how we are sundered, turning us into spectators of its world and our own. However, *A Midsummer Night's Dream* ends with the promise of mending, as if its actors really would join, construct, repair, and weave together rather than just teaching us the parts they have conned. Puck's epilogue in its sixteen short lines twice offers to "mend" and twice promises "amends." We should consider the interplay of these words, how they rhyme with each other and with the ends of the play:

> If we shadows have offended,
> Think but this, and all is mended—
> That you have but slumbered here
> While these visions did appear.
> And this weak and idle theme,
> No more yielding than a dream,
> Gentles, do not reprehend.
> If you pardon, we will mend.
>
> (5.1.412–19)

How could the theater mend us, join us together as it shows us that we are parts and apart? Could it form a union in partition, as if what kept us separate hinged on what assembled us? In one sense it is the place of theater to transfix its spectators in one spot, to make them stand together—both literally and through its figures by joining their minds in a common vision and point of view. This collective stance is what is strange and admirable about what passes for a dream one midsummer's night. Theseus denies the "fantasies" (5.1.5) the lovers wake up with, but Hippolyta remarks on the strange "compact" of imagination the lovers seem to share:

> But all the story of the night told over,
> And all their minds transfigured so together,
> More witnesseth than fancy's images
> And grows to something of great constancy.
>
> (5.1.23–26)

Hippolyta's description of a concord of minds that seem to stand together is also the dream of theater: that we could be joined together in a collective hallucination, that figures could be carried across and visions shared. The dream of theater is that particular stories, images, and minds could "grow" "so together" that they would seem like Hermia and Helena, who "grew together . . . seeming parted, / But yet an union in partition" (3.2.208–10).

After the lovers awaken into a double world that still has the air of dreaming about it, Demetrius proposes, "let us recount our dreams" (4.1.198). According to Hippolyta, they recount them and add them together. However, Demetrius' proposal is also Bottom's cue to awaken from his dream and declare his famous lines: "I have had a most rare vision. I have had a dream, past the wit of any man to say what dream it was. Man is but an ass if he go about to expound this dream"

(4.1.203–5). *A Midsummer Night's Dream* leaves open the question of whether we can recount or expound our dreams; perhaps it was the threat that Bottom and not Demetrius was right that caused Freud to practically ignore this play in his writing. But *A Midsummer Night's Dream* both reminds us and asks us to forget about the epistemological problem that dreams raise and stand for. We might be able to tell our dreams (or translate them into ballets or plays; this may mean to act them out), but we cannot know the dreams of other people. The magic of the play is that separate minds appear to be transfigured together; dreams (or what seem like dreams) appear to be shared. This is the dream that will mend the spectators of the play if they think that they have slumbered and witnessed the same visions and dream.

Yet Puck ends by reminding us that this is also a dream that calls for amends: "We will make amends ere long; . . . Give me your hands, if we be friends. / And Robin shall restore amends" (5.1.423–27). Why must he restore amends? The play, in part, has recounted our losses, but it has also robbed us. Recall that when Theseus prefigures the opening of Puck's epilogue by calling actors "shadows," he says that "the worst are no worse, if imagination amend them," to which Hippolyta rejoins, "It must be your imagination then, and not theirs" (5.1. 209–11). We have seen the willfulness of Theseus' imagination, the power of his projections, Hippolyta's revision of her husband's claim recalls that the interplay of imaginations in the play is often portrayed as a struggle. Spectators are expected to work their imaginations upon a play (this is what the prologue to *Henry V* requests of us), but at the end of *A Midsummer Night's Dream* we are faced with the possibility that we have been worked upon, that we are owed amends because *our* imaginations have been amended: changed, altered, revised. Have we found to our cost that a vision and a dream have been reduced to an unmanageable reality? Or have we found to our cost that a vision has been imposed upon us, that impressions of our fantasies have been stolen? What does it mean that we have slumbered? When Puck causes Helena to slumber, she speaks of "sleep" as that which will "steal me awhile from my own company" (3.2.436). What does it mean that the dream we are told we have witnessed is said to have an "idle theme" (5.1.416)? It is with the flower called "love-in-idleness" (2.1.168) that Oberon makes Titania render up her page to him by streaking her eyes and filling her with fantasies. Have we lost ourselves or the figures we imagined for ourselves? What are we to think of this dream that for a while has reduced us to silence and filled our minds with airy shapes and fantasies? As spectators—and as readers—we must wonder what hapens when we see with someone else's eyes, allow ourselves to become the blank page upon which an author imprints characters, a play representations. The marriage of true minds that is the dream of theater presents the double prospect that it might mar us as it mends us, steal as it restores. What does theater's figuring or disfiguring add up to? Can theater's "transfiguring" mediate between or synthesize figuring and disfiguring? What do we exchange for our visions?

VI

We have seen that *A Midsummer Night's Dream* dramatizes an economy of exchange, as if, like the *Sonnets,* its figures marked various registers with the expenses of loss and possesion. The terms and imagery of theft are set down in the first scene, which pictures the "traffic in women" (to use Emma Goldman's phrase) upon which men for so long have founded their societies; and throughout the play, characters are figured as merchandise or stolen goods. (Hermia, Lysander, Helena, Demetrius, Egeus, Oberon, and Titania each "steal" or are stolen from or are stolen in the course of the play.) The figure for these character-commodities is the child who rivals Hermia as the most contested "property" in the play: the changeling boy that Titania is accused of having "stolen" (2.1.22). (According to folk tales, fairies stole lovely children and left deformed "changelings" in exchange; this boy is the changeling the fairies took, not left behind.) When Titania insists to Oberon that "the fairyland buys not the child of me" (2.1.122), she is perpetuating rather than rejecting terms that inscribe people in a system of economic relations. Her monologue pictures the boy as "merchandise" which his mother's womb, like a trader's ship, was "rich with" (2.1.127–34). The changeling comes to represent all of the characters in the play who are traded or fought over as property. It also shows us that the other characters are changelings in the sense that the play's plot revolves around their exchanges: their substitutions and their interchangeability. Demetrius, Lysander, Hermia, and Helena all exchange one another (are exchanged for one another) in almost every possible switch and combination. Bottom, too, is "changed" and "translated" (3.1.,103,107). In becoming a disfigured substitute for Titania's changeling bcy, he becomes both a changeling for himself (a monster left in his own place) and a changeling for the changeling (which Titania has been tricked into exchanging). The changeling boy is mysteriously absent in *A Midsummer Night's Dream*, but in a sense he is everywhere; the play casts its characters as changelings.

We also could say that the play is performed by changelings because that is what actors are. For Shakespeare's spectators, the term "changeling" would have been a synonym for someone Protean who would not stay the same from one moment to the next. This is precisely the "ontological subversiveness" (as Jonas Barish has called it [in a 1966 article on anti-theatrical prejudice]) that actors were condemned for in Elizabethan England. Actors take others' parts and places; they exchange themselves for others, substitute others for themselves. This is further compounded in *A Midsummer Night's Dream* because characters often seem to be changed into actors: as parts and partners are exchanged and mixed up, individual characters seem reduced to parts or roles. We watch changelings portray changelings.

In another sense, changelings are everywhere in the play because they fill its pages and dialogue: they are its figures of speech. The figures that Titania employs to tell the changeling's story enact and figure exchange in various senses. Describing herself on the shore with the woman who is pregnant with the boy, she tropes the ships to see their "sails conceive / And grow big-bellied with the wanton wind" (2.1.128–29). Then the metaphor doubles or reverses—it is exchanged—as Titania tropes the woman to see her "rich" with her own human cargo, just as the woman tropes herself to "imitate" the ships and "sail upon the land / To fetch me trifles, and return again, / As from a voyage, rich with merchandise" (2.1.313–34). The woman and the ships stand for each other, exchanging properties in a double sense. If we recognize the act of carrying and trading cargo performed by these literal and figurative ships to be *transport* (as in *metaphérein*) then we see that these double metaphors both dramatize and figure *metaphor* as they transfer, transfigure, exchange, and carry across. Born of this mirror of metaphors, destined to be switched, substituted, and exchanged, the changeling is also a trope for tropes. It makes sense, then, that in *The Arte of English Poesie*, published in 1589, Puttenham invents a rhetorical category called "Figures of Exchange" and names one of those figures "the Changeling." Puttenham refers to exactly the sort of constructions the mechanicals make—"a play with . . . wordes, using a wrong construction for a right, and an absurd for a sensible, by manner of exchange"—but we can see that in a sense all tropes act as changelings. The changeling figures figures.

That Puttenham uses "changeling" to mean something ill-formed which appears in the place of something fair reminds us that in *A Midsummer Night's Dream* the changeling is not the disfigured child. Appropriately, the play ends with a blessing by Oberon, who has authored many of the play's exchanges and deformations in pursuit of his page, to insure for the newly married couples that

> the blots of Nature's hand
> Shall not in their issue stand.
> Never mole, harelip, nor scar,
> Nor mark prodigious, such as are
> Despised in nativity,
> Shall upon their children be.
>
> (5.1.398–403)

Prefacing Puck's appeal for our blessing and his promise of amends, Oberon's reprise of the figure of the changeling might remind us of the questions facing us at the end of the play. We might wonder again if we who have rendered up the pages of our imaginations in exchange for the play leave the theater free (or freed) from blots or disfigurement. This is what worried us as we let the play imprint its figures on us, risking change and amending. Have we been stolen and left as changelings? I asked the question: What do we exchange for our visions? I meant to suggest that we both give up visions in this exchange *and* get visions in return. In this sense the exchange of visions might be seen as an alternative to the theft of visions in the play. What is at stake appears to be our visions of ourselves: we would not be forced to look with someone else's eyes, to submit to the tyranny of someone else's view or imagination of us.

Yet how do we see ourselves? In the theater, we see ourselves as changelings: capable of seeing ourselves on the stage, substituted for by actors whose parts we take in acts of sympathy or identification. We allow actors to stand as changelings for us, whether or not we recognize them as they present or disfigure us, as they act our parts. In this sense we see with "parted eye" and "everything seems double"; we both take their eyes and see for ourselves. The theater is like the "dark night" that, in Hermia's words, "from the eye his function takes"; it may "impair the seeing sense," but it offers other senses "double recompense" (3.2.177–80). It keeps us in the dark, but it offers to show us ourselves—doubled. The double recompense in this play of double visions would be to learn how to see and to learn how to see others. It is this double vision that Theseus, Egeus, and Oberon in their single-mindedness cannot know. Recall that Hermia—whose eyes are "blessed and attractive" (2.1.91) "lodestars" (1.1.183)—is asked by Helena: "O, teach me how you look" (1.1.192). To teach one how you look might be the alternative to the tyranny that forces someone to see with another's eyes or to assume a character that someone else figures and impresses. To learn how you look would be to learn what you look like and to learn how you see: both to take your eyes and to let you see yourself. This is the recompense if you let someone take your eyes and see the figure of yourself. If we risk seeing our visions disfigured—if we figure our visions in order to see them, despite the cost—this is only because we cannot be represented; we can only be believed. To learn this exchange of visions would be to release others from the roles we cast them in, to permit them to stop being changelings. Only when these visions are double—each of us learning how to look—will we be able to recognize disfiguring and provide it in exchange another sense. *A Midsummer Night's Dream* figures these relations as loss, and in a sense it inscribes us in it. The play, however, might teach us how to look. If we will let one of Bottom's lines echo apart from its comic context, we can hear the admonishment, warning, and offer of vision that the play addresses to its spectators: "let the audience look to their eyes" (1.2.22).

The Bottomless Dream

Northrop Frye

Elizabethan literature began as a provincial development of a Continent-centred literature, and it's full of imitations and translations from French, Italian and Latin. But the dramatists practically had to rediscover drama, as soon as, early in Elizabeth's reign, theatres with regular performances of plays on a thrust stage began to evolve out of temporary constructions in dining halls and courtyards. There was some influence from Italian theatre, and some of the devices in *Twelfth Night* reminded one spectator, who kept a diary, of Italian sources. There was also the influence of the half-improvised *commedia dell'arte,* which I'll speak of later. Behind these Italian influences were the Classical plays from which the Italian ones partly derived.

For tragedy there were not many precedents, apart from the Latin plays of Seneca, whose tragedies may not have been actually intended for the stage. Seneca is a powerful influence behind Shakespeare's earliest tragedy, *Titus Andronicus,* and there are many traces of him elsewhere. In comedy, though, there were about two dozen Latin plays available, six by Terence, the rest by Plautus. These had been adapted from the Greek writers of what we call New Comedy, to distinguish it from the Old Comedy of Aristophanes, which was full of personal attacks and allusions to actual people and events. The best known of these Greek New Comedy writers was Menander, whose work, except for one complete play recently discovered, has come

From *Northrop Frye on Shakespeare,* edited by Robert Sandler. © 1986 by Northrop Frye. Yale University Press, 1986.

117

down to us only in fragments. Menander was a sententious, aphoristic writer, and one of his aphorisms ("evil communications corrupt good manners") was quoted by Paul in the New Testament. Terence carried on this sententious style, and we find some famous proverbs in him, such as "I am a man, and nothing human is alien to me." When we hear a line like "The course of true love never did run smooth" in *A Midsummer Night's Dream,* familiar to many people who don't know the play, we can see that the same tradition is still going strong. And later on, when we hear Bottom mangling references to Paul's epistles, we may feel that we're going around in a circle.

New Comedy, in Plautus, and Terence, usually sets up a situation that's the opposite of the one that the audience would recognize as the "right" one. Let's say a young man loves a young woman, and vice versa, but their love is blocked by parents who want suitors or brides with more money. That's the first part. The second part consists of the complications that follow, and in a third and last part the opening situation is turned inside out, usually through some gimmick in the plot, such as the discovery that the heroine was kidnapped in infancy by pirates, or that she was exposed on a hillside and rescued by a shepherd, but that her social origin is quite respectable enough for her to marry the hero. The typical characters in such a story are the young man (*adulescens*), a heavy father (sometimes called *senex iratus,* because he often goes into terrible rages when he's thwarted), and a "tricky slave" (*dolosus servus*), who helps out the young man with some clever scheme. If you look at the plays of Molière, you'll see these characters over and over again, and the tricky servant is still there in the Figaro operas of Rossini and Mozart—and in Wodehouse's Jeeves. Often the roles of young man and young woman are doubled: in a play of Plautus, adapted by Shakespeare in *The Comedy of Errors,* the young men are twin brothers, and Shakespeare adds a pair of twin servants.

In Shakespeare's comedies we often get two heroines as well: we have Rosalind and Celia in *As You Like It,* Hero and Beatrice in *Much Ado about Nothing,* Olivia and Viola in *Twelfth Night,* Julia and Silvia in *The Two Gentlemen of Verona,* Helena and Hermia in this play. It's a natural inference that there were two boys in Shakespeare's company who were particularly good at female roles. If so, one seems to have been noticeably taller than the other. In *As You Like It* we're not sure which was the taller one—the indications are contradictory—but here they're an almost comic-strip contrast, Helena being long and drizzly and Hermia short and spitty.

Shakespeare's comedies are far more complex than the Roman ones, but the standard New Comedy structure usually forms part of their actions. To use Puck's line, the Jacks generally get their Jills in the end (or the Jills get their Jacks, which in fact happens more often). But he makes certain modifications in the standard plot, and makes them fairly consistently. He doesn't seem to like plots that turn on tricky-servant schemes. He does have smart or cheeky servants often enough, like Lancelot Gobbo in *The Merchant of Venice,* and they make the complacent soliloquies that are common in the role, but they seldom affect the action. Puck and Ariel come nearest, and we notice that neither is a human being and neither acts on his own. Then again, Shakespeare generally plays down the outwitting and baffling of age by youth: the kind of action suggested by the title of a play of Middleton's, *A Trick to Catch the Old-One,* is rare in Shakespeare. The most prominent example is the ganging up on Shylock in *The Merchant of Venice* that lets his daughter Jessica marry Lorenzo. Even that leaves a rather sour taste in our mouths, and the sour taste is part of the play, not just part of our different feelings about stage Jews. In the late romances, especially *Pericles* and *The Winter's Tale,* the main comic resolution concerns older people, who are united or reconciled after a long separation. Even in this play, while we start out with a standard New Comedy situation in which lovers are forbidden to marry but succeed in doing so all the same, it's the older people, Theseus and Hippolyta, who are at the centre of the action, and we could add to this the reconciling of Oberon and Titania.

In the Roman plays there's a general uniformity of social rank: the characters are usually ordinary middle-class people with their servants. The settings are also uniform and consistent: they're not "realistic," but the action is normally urban, taking place on the street in front of the houses of the main characters, and there certainly isn't much of mystery, romance, fairies, magic or mythology (except for farcical treatments of it like Plautus's *Amphitryon*). I've spoken [elsewhere] of the highbrows in Shakespeare's time who thought that Classical prece-dents were models to be imitated, and that you weren't writing ac-cording to the proper rules if you introduced kings or princes or dukes into comedies, as Shakespeare is constantly doing, or if you introduced the incredible or mysterious, such as fairies or magic. Some of Shake-speare's younger contemporaries, notably Ben Johnson, keep more closely to Classical precedent, and Jonson tells us that he reguarly follows nature, and that some other people like Shakespeare don't. Shakespeare never fails to introduce something mysterious or hard to believe into his comedies, and in doing so he's following the precedents set, not by the Classical writers, but by his immediate predecessors.

These predecessors included in particular three writers of comedy, Peele, Greene and Lyly. Peele's *Old Wives' Tale* is full of themes from folk tales; in Greene's *Friar Bacon and Friar Bungay* the central character is a magician, and in his *James IV*, while there's not much about the Scottish king of that name, there's a chorus character called Oberon, the king of the fairies; in Lyly's *Endimion* the main story retells the Classical myth of Endymion, the youth beloved by the goddess of the moon. These are examples of the type of romance-comedy that Shakespeare followed. Shakespeare keeps the three-part structure of the Roman plays, but immensely expands the second part, and makes it a prolonged episode of confused identity. Sometimes the heroine disguises herself as a boy; sometimes the action moves into a charmed area, often a magic wood like the one in this play, where the ordinary laws of nature don't quite apply.

If we ask why this type of early Elizabethan comedy should have been the type Shakespeare used, there are many answers, but one relates to the audience. *A Midsummer Night's Dream* has the general appearance of a play designed for a special festive occasion, when the Queen herself might well be present. In such a play one would expect an occasional flattering allusion to her, and it looks as though we have one when Oberon refers to an "imperial votaress" in a speech to Puck. The Queen was also normally very tolerant about the often bungling attempts to entertain her when she made her progressions through the country, and so the emphasis placed on Theseus's courtesy to the Quince company may also refer to her, even if he is male. But if there were an allusion to her, it would have to be nothing more than that.

Even today novelists have to put statements into their books that no real people are being alluded to, and in Shakespeare's day anything that even looked like such an allusion, beyond the conventional compliments, could be dangerous. Three of Shakespeare's contemporaries did time in jail for putting into a play a couple of sentences that sounded like satire on the Scotsmen coming to England in the train of James I, and worse things, like cutting off ears and noses, could be threatened. I make this point because every so often some director or critic gets the notion that this play is really all about Queen Elizabeth, or that certain characters, such as Titania, refer to her. The consequences to Shakespeare's dramatic career if the Queen had believed that she was being publicly represented as having a love affair with a jackass are something we fortunately don't have to think about.

An upper-class audience is inclined to favour romance and fantasy in its entertainment, because the idealizing element in such romance confirms its own image of itself. And whatever an upper-class audience likes is probably going to be what a middle-class audience will like too. If this play was adapted to, or commissioned for, a special court performance, it would be the kind of thing Theseus is looking for at the very beginning of the play, when he tells his master of revels, Philostrate, to draw up a list of possible entertainments. One gets an impression of sparseness about what Philostrate has collected, even if Theseus doesn't read the whole list; but however that may be, the Peter Quince play has something of the relation to the nuptials of Theseus that Shakespeare's play would have had to whatever occasion it was used for. We notice that the reason for some of the absurdities in the Quince play come from the actors' belief that court ladies are unimaginably fragile and delicate: they will swoon at the sight of Snug the joiner as a lion unless it is carefully explained that he isn't really a lion. The court ladies belong to the Quince players' fairyland: Shakespeare knew far more about court ladies than they did, but he also realized that court ladies and gentlemen had some affinity, as an audience, with fairyland.

This play retains the three parts of a normal comedy that I mentioned earlier: a first part in which an absurd, unpleasant or irrational situation is set up; a second part of confused identity and personal complications; a third part in which the plot gives a shake and twist and everything comes right in the end. In the opening of this play we meet an irrational law, of a type we often do meet at the beginning of a Shakespeare comedy: the law of Athens that decrees death or perpetual imprisonment in a convent for any young woman who marries without her father's consent. Here the young woman is Hermia, who loves Lysander, and the law is invoked by her father, Egeus, who prefers Demetrius. Egeus is a senile old fool who clearly doesn't love his daughter, and is quite reconciled to seeing her executed or imprisoned. What he loves is his own possession of his daughter, which carries the right to bestow her on a man of his choice as a proxy for himself. He makes his priorities clear in a speech later in the play:

> They would have stol'n away, they would, Demetrius,
> Thereby to have defeated you and me:

> You of your wife, and me of my consent,
> Of my consent that she should be your wife.
>
> (4.1.155–58)

Nevertheless Theseus admits that the law is what Egeus says it is, and also emphatically says that the law must be enforced, and that he himself has no power to abrogate it. We meet this situation elsewhere in Shakespeare: at the beginning of *The Comedy of Errors,* with its law that in Ephesus all visitors from Syracuse are to be beheaded, and in *The Merchant of Venice,* with the law that upholds Shylock's bond. In all three cases the person in authority declares that he has no power to alter the law, and in all three cases he eventually does. As it turns out that Theseus is a fairly decent sort, we may like to rationalize this scene by assuming that he is probably going to talk privately with Egeus and Demetrius (as in fact he says he is) and work out a more humane solution. But he gives Hermia no loophole: he merely repeats the threats to her life and freedom. Then he adjourns the session:

> Come, my Hippolyta—what cheer, my love?
>
> (1.1.122)

which seems a clear indication that Hippolyta, portrayed throughout the play as a person of great common sense, doesn't like the set-up at all.

We realize that sooner or later Lysander and Hermia will get out from under this law and be united in spite of Egeus. Demetrius and Helena, who are the doubling figures, are in an unresolved situation: Helena loves Demetrius, but Demetrius has only, in the Victorian phrase, trifled with her affections. In the second part we're in the fairy wood at night, where identities become, as we think, hopelessly confused. At dawn Theseus and Hippolyta, accompanied by Egeus, enter the wood to hunt. By that time the Demetrius-Helena situation has cleared up, and because of that Theseus feels able to overrule Egeus and allow the two marriages to go ahead. At the beginning Lysander remarks to Hermia that the authority of Athenian law doesn't extend as far as the wood, but apparently it does; Theseus is there, in full charge, and it is in the wood that he makes the decision that heads the play toward its happy ending. At the same time the solidifying of the Demetrius-Helena relationship was the work of Oberon. We can hardly avoid the feeling not only that Theseus is overruling Egeus's will, but that his own will has been overruled too, by fairies of whom he knows nothing and in whose existence he doesn't believe.

If we look at the grouping of characters in each of the three parts, this feeling becomes still stronger. In the opening scene we have Theseus, Egeus and an unwilling Hippolyta in the centre, symbolizing parental authority and the inflexibility of law, with three of the four young people standing before them. Before long we meet the fourth, Helena. In the second part the characters are grouped in different places within the wood, for the most part separated from one another. In one part of the wood are the lovers; in another are the processions of the quarrelling king and queen of the fairies; in still another Peter Quince and his company are rehearsing their play. Finally the remaining group, Theseus, Hippolyta and Egeus, appear with the sunrise. In the first part no one doubts that Theseus is the supreme ruler over the court of Athens; in the second part no one doubts that Oberon is king of the fairies and directs what goes on in the magic wood.

In the third and final part the characters, no longer separated from one another, are very symmetrically arranged. Peter Quince and his company are in the most unlikely spot, in the middle, and the centre of attention; around them sit Theseus and Hippolyta and the four now reconciled lovers. The play ends; Theseus calls for a retreat to bed, and then the fairies come in for the final blessing of the house, forming a circumference around all the others. They are there for the sake of Theseus and Hippolyta, but their presence suggests that Theseus is not as supremely the ruler of his own world as he seemed to be at first.

A Midsummer Night's Dream seems to be one of the relatively few plays that Shakespeare made up himself, without much help from sources. Two sources he did use were tragic stories that are turned into farce here. One was the story of Pyramus and Thisbe from Ovid, which the Quince company is attempting to tell, and which is used for more than just the Quince play. The other was Chaucer's *Knight's Tale,* from which Shakespeare evidently took the names of Theseus, Hippolyta and Philostrate, and which is a gorgeous but very sombre story of the fatal rivalry of two men over a woman. So far as this theme appears in the play, it is in the floundering of Lysander and Demetrius after first Hermia and then Helena, bemused with darkness and Puck's love drugs. I spoke [elsewhere] of the relation of the original Pyramus and Thisbe story to *Romeo and Juliet,* and the theme of the *Knight's Tale* appears vestigally in that play too, in the fatal duel of Romeo and Paris. I spoke also of the role of the oxymoron as a figure of speech in *Romeo and Juliet,* the self-contradictory figure that's appropriate to a tragedy of love and death. That too appears as

farce in this play, when Theseus reads the announcement of the Quince
play:

> Merry and tragical? Tedious and brief?
> That is hot ice, and wondrous strange snow!
> How shall we find the concord of this discord?
>
> (5.1.58–60)

Why is this play called *A Midsummer Night's Dream*? Apparently the
main action in the fairy wood takes place on the eve of May Day; at
any rate, when Theseus and Hippolyta enter with the rising sun, they
discover the four lovers, and Theseus says:

> No doubt they rose up early to observe
> The rite of May.
>
> (4.1.131–32)

We call the time of the summer solstice, in the third week of June,
"midsummer," although in our calendars it's the beginning of summer. That's because originally there were only three seasons, summer,
autumn and winter: summer then included spring and began in March.
A thirteenth-century song begins "sumer is i-cumen in," generally
modernized, to keep the metre, as "summer is a-coming in," but it
doesn't mean that: it means "spring is here." The Christian calendar
finally established the celebration of the birth of Christ at the winter
solstice, and made a summer solstice date (June 24) the feast day of
John the Baptist. This arrangement, according to the Fathers, symbolized John's remark in the Gospels on beholding Christ: "He must
increase, but I must decrease." Christmas Eve was a beneficent time,
when evil spirits had no power; St. John's Eve was perhaps more
ambiguous, and there was a common phrase, "midsummer madness,"
used by Olivia in *Twelfth Night,* a play named after the opposite end of
the year. Still, it was a time when spirits of nature, whether benevolent
or malignant, might be supposed to be abroad.

There were also two other haunted "eves," of the first of Novem-
ber and of the first of May. These take us back to a still earlier time,
when animals were brought in from the pasture at the beginning of
winter, with a slaughter of those that couldn't be kept to feed, and
when they were let out again at the beginning of spring. The first of
these survives in our Hallowe'en, but May Day eve is no longer
thought of much as a spooky time, although in Germany, where it was
called "Walpurgis night," the tradition that witches held an assembly

on a mountain at that time lasted much longer, and comes into Goethe's *Faust*. In *Faust* the scene with the witches is followed by something called "The Golden Wedding of Oberon and Titania," which has nothing to do with Shakespeare's play, but perhaps indicates a connection in Goethe's mind between it and the first of May.

In Shakespeare's time, as Theseus's remark indicates, the main emphasis on the first of May fell on a sunrise service greeting the day with songs. All the emphasis was on hope and cheerfulness. Shakespeare evidently doesn't want to force a specific date on us: it may be May Day eve, but all we can be sure of is that it's later than St. Valentine's Day in mid-February, the day when traditionally the birds start copulating, and we could have guessed that anyway. The general idea is that we have gone through the kind of night when spirits are powerful but not necessarily malevolent. Evil spirits, as we learn from the opening scene of *Hamlet,* are forced to disappear at dawn, and the fact that this is also true of the Ghost of Hamlet's father sows a terrible doubt in Hamlet's mind. Here we have Puck, or more accurately Robin Goodfellow *the* puck. Pucks were a category of spirits who were often sinister, and the Puck of this play is clearly mischievous. But we are expressly told by Oberon that the fairies of whom he's the king are "spirits of another sort," not evil and not restricted to darkness.

So the title of the play simply emphasizes the difference between the two worlds of the action, the waking world of Theseus's court and the fairy world of Oberon. Let's go back to the three parts of the comic action: the opening situation hostile to true love, the middle part of dissolving identities and the final resolution. The first part contains a threat of possible death to Hermia. Similar threats are found in other Shakespeare comedies: in *The Comedy of Errors* a death sentence hangs over a central character until nearly the end of the play. This comic structure fits inside a pattern of death, disappearance and return that's far wider in scope than theatrical comedy. We find it even in the central story of Christianity, with its Friday of death, Saturday of disappearance and Sunday of return. Scholars who have studied this pattern in religion, mythology and legend think it derives from observing the moon waning, then disappearing, then reappearing as a new moon.

At the opening Theseus and Hippolyta have agreed to hold their wedding at the next new moon, now four days off. They speak of four days, although the rhetorical structure runs in threes: Hippolyta is wooed, won and wed "With pomp, with triumph and with revelling."

(This reading depends also on a reasonable, if not certain, emendation: "new" for "now" in the tenth line.) Theseus compares his impatience to the comedy situation of a young man waiting for someone older to die and leave him money. The Quince company discover from an almanac that there will be moonshine on the night that they will be performing, but apparently there is not enough, and so they introduce a character called Moonshine. His appearance touches off a very curious reprise of the opening dialogue. Hippolyta says "I am aweary of this moon: would he would change!" and Theseus answers that he seems to be on the wane, "but yet, in courtesy . . . we must stay the time." It's as though this ghastly play contains in miniature, and caricature, the themes of separation, postponement, and confusions of reality and fantasy that have organized the play surrounding it.

According to the indications in the text, the night in the wood should be a moonless night, but in fact there are so many references to the moon that it seems to be still there, even though obscured by clouds. It seems that this wood is a fairyland with its own laws of time and space, a world where Oberon has just blown in from India and where Puck can put a girdle round the earth in forty minutes. So it's not hard to accept such a world as an antipodal one, like the world of dreams itself, which, although we make it fit into our waking-time schedules, still keeps to its own quite different rhythms. A curious image of Hermia's involving the moon has echoes of this; she's protesting that she will never believe Lysander unfaithful:

> I'll believe as soon
> This whole earth may be bored, and that the moon
> May through the centre creep, and so displease
> Her brother's noontide with th'Antipodes.
>
> (3.2.52–55)

A modern reader might think of the opening of "The Walrus and the Carpenter." The moon, in any case, seems to have a good deal to do with both worlds. In the opening scene Lysander speaks of Demetrius as "this spotted and inconstant man," using two common epithets for the moon, and in the last act Theseus speaks of "the lunatic, the lover and the poet," where "lunatic" has its full Elizabethan force of "moonstruck."

The inhabitants of the wood-world are the creatures of legend and folk tale and mythology and abandoned belief. Theseus regards them as projections of the human imagination, and as having a purely subjective existence. The trouble is that we don't know the extent of our own minds, or what's in that mental world that we half create and half perceive, in Wordsworth's phrase. The tiny fairies that wait on Bottom—Mustardseed and Peaseblossom and the rest—come from Celtic fairy lore, as does the Queen Mab of Mercutio's speech, who also had tiny fairies in her train. Robin Goodfellow is more Anglo-Saxon and Teutonic. His propitiatory name, "Goodfellow," indicates that he could be dangerous, and his fairy friend says that one of his amusements is to "Mislead night-wanderers, laughing at their harm." A famous book a little later than Shakespeare, Robert Burton's *Anatomy of Melancholy*, mentions fire spirits who mislead travellers with illusions, and says "We commonly call them pucks." The fairy world clearly would not do as a democracy: there has to be a king in charge like Oberon, who will see that Puck's rather primitive sense of humour doesn't get too far out of line.

The gods and other beings of Classical mythology belong in the same half-subjective, half-autonomous world. I've spoken of the popularity of Ovid's *Metamorphoses* for poets: this, in Ovid's opening words, is a collection of stories of "bodies changed to new forms." Another famous Classical metamorphosis is the story of Apuleius about a man turned into an ass by enchantment, and of course this theme enters the present play when Bottom is, as Quince says, "translated." In Classical mythology one central figure was the goddess that Robert Graves, whose book I'll mention [elsewhere], calls the "white goddess" or the "triple will." This goddess had three forms: one in heaven, where she was the goddess of the moon and was called Phoebe or Cynthia or Luna; one on earth, where she was Diana, the virgin huntress of the forest, called Titania once in Ovid; and one below the earth, where she was the witch-goddess Hecate. Puck speaks of "Hecates' triple team" at the end of the play. References to Diana and Cynthia by the poets of the time usually involved some allusion to the virgin queen Elizabeth (they always ignored Hecate in such contexts). As I said, the Queen seems to be alluded to here, but in a way that kicks her upstairs, so to speak: she's on a level far above all the "lunatic" goings-on below.

Titania in this play is not Diana: Diana and her moon are in Theseus's world, and stand for the sterility that awaits Hermia if she disobeys her father, when she will have to become Diana's nun, "Chanting faint hymns to the cold fruitless moon." The wood of this play is erotic, not virginal: Puck is contemptuous of Lysander's lying so far away from Hermia, not realizing that this was just Hermia being maidenly. According to Oberon, Cupid was an inhabitant of this wood, and had shot his erotic arrow at the "imperial votaress," but it glanced off her and fell on a white flower, turning it red. The parabola taken by this arrow outlines the play's world, so to speak: the action takes place under this red and white arch. One common type of Classical myth deals with a "dying god," as he's called now, a male figure who is killed when still a youth, and whose blood stains a white flower and turns it red or purple. Shakespeare had written the story of one of these gods in his narrative poem *Venus and Adonis,* where he makes a good deal of the stained flower:

> No flower was nigh, no grass, herb, leaf, or weed,
> But stole his blood and seem'd with him to bleed.

The story of Pyramus and Thisbe is another such story: Pyramus's blood stains the mulberry and turns it red. In Ovid's account, when Pyramus stabs himself the blood spurts out in an arc on the flower. This may be where Shakespeare got the image that he puts to such very different use.

Early in the play we come upon Oberon and Titania quarrelling over the custody of a human boy, and we are told that because of their quarrel the weather has been unusually foul. The implication is that the fairies are spirits of the elements, and that nature and human life are related in many ways that are hidden from ordinary consciousness. But it seems clear that Titania does not have the authority that she thinks she has: Oberon puts her under the spell of having to fall in love with Bottom with his ass's head, and rescues the boy for his own male entourage. There are other signs that Titania is a possessive and entangling spirit—she says to Bottom:

> Out of this wood do not desire to go;
> Thou shalt remain here, whether thou wilt or no.
>
> (3.1.143–44)

The relationship of Oberon and Titania forms a counterpoint with that of Theseus and Hippolyta in the other world. It appears that Titania has been a kind of guardian spirit to Hippolyta and Oberon to Theseus. Theseus gives every sign of settling down into a solidly married man, now that he has subdued the most formidable woman in the world, the Queen of the Amazons. But his record before that was a very bad one, with rapes and desertions in it: even as late as T. S. Eliot we read about his "perjured sails." Oberon blames his waywardness on Titania's influence, and Titania's denial does not sound very convincing. Oberon's ascendancy over Titania, and Theseus's over Hippolyta, seem to symbolize some aspect of the emerging comic resolution.

Each world has a kind of music, or perhaps rather "harmony," that is characteristic of it. That of the fairy wood is represented by the song of the mermaid described by Oberon to Puck. This is a music that commands the elements of the "sublunary" world below the moon; it quiets the sea, but there is a hint of a lurking danger in it, a siren's magic call that draws some of the stars out of their proper spheres in heaven, as witches according to tradition can call down the moon. There is danger everywhere in that world for mortals who stay there too long and listen to too much of its music. When the sun rises and Theseus and Hippolyta enter the wood, they talk about the noise of hounds in this and other huntings. Hippolyta says:

> never did I hear
> Such gallant chiding; for, besides the groves,
> The Skies, the fountains, every region near
> Seem'd all one mutual cry; I never heard
> So musical a discord, such sweet thunder.
>
> (4.1.113–17)

It would not occur to us to describe a cry of hounds as a kind of symphony orchestra, but then we do not have the mystique of a Renaissance prince about hunting. Both forms of music fall far short of the supreme harmony of the spheres described in the fifth act of *Th Merchant of Venice:* Oberon might know something about that, but not Puck, who can't see the "imperial votaress." Neither, probably, could Theseus.

So the wood-world has affinities with what we call the unconscious or subconscious part of the mind: a part below the reason's encounter with objective reality, and yet connected with the hidden creative powers of the mind. Left to Puck or even Titania, it's a world of illusion, random desires and shifting identities. With Oberon in charge, it becomes the world in which those profound choices are made that decide the course of life, and also (we pick this up later) the world from which inspiration comes to the poet. The lovers wake up still dazed wih metamorphosis; as Demetrius says:

> These things seem small and undistinguishable,
> Like far-off mountains turnèd into clouds.
>
> (4.1.186–87)

But the comic crystalization has taken place, and for the fifth act we go back to Theseus's court to sort out the various things that have come out of the wood.

Theseus takes a very rational and common-sense view of the lovers' story, but he makes it clear that the world of the wood is the world of the poet as well as the lover and the lunatic. His very remarkable speech uses the words "apprehend" and "comprehend" each twice. In the oridnary world we apprehend with our senses and comprehend with our reason; what the poet apprehends are moods or emotions, like joy, and what he uses for comprehension is some story or character to account for the emotion:

> Such tricks hath strong imagination,
> That if it would but apprehend some joy,
> It comprehends some bringer of that joy
>
> (5.1.18–20)

Theseus is here using the word "imagination" in its common Elizabethan meaning, which we express by the word "imaginary," something alleged to be that isn't. In spite of himself, though, the word is taking on the more positive sense of our "imaginative," the sense of the creative power developed centuries later by Blake and Coleridge. So far as I can make out from the OED, this more positive sense of the word in English practically begins here. Hippolyta is shrewder and less defensive than Theseus, and what she says takes us a great deal further:

> But all the story of the night, told over,
> And all their minds transfigur'd so together,
> More witnesseth than fancy's images,
> And grows to something of great constancy;
> But howsoever, strange and admirable.
>
> (5.1.23–27)

Theseus doesn't believe their story, but Hippolyta sees that something has happened to them, whatever their story. The word "transfigured" means that there can be metamorphosis upward as well as downward, a creative transforming into a higher consciousness as well as the reduction from the conscious to the unconscious that we read about in Ovid. Besides, the story has a consistency to it that doesn't sound like the disjointed snatches of incoherent minds. If you want disjointing and incoherence, just listen to the play that's coming up. And yet the Quince play is a triumph of sanity in its way: it tells you that the roaring lion is only Snug the joiner, for example. It's practically a parody of Theseus's view of reality, with its "imagination" that takes a bush for a bear in the dark. There's a later exchange when Hippolyta complains that the play is silly, and Theseus says:

> The best in this kind are but shadows; and the worst are no
> worse, if imagination amend them
>
> (5.1.209–10)

Hippolyta retorts: "It must be your imagination, then, and not theirs." Here "imagination" has definitely swung over to meaning something positive and creative. What Hippolyta says implies that the audience has a creative role in every play; that's one reason why Puck, coming out for the Epilogue when the audience is supposed to applaud, repeats two of Theseus's words:

> If we shadows have offended,
> Think but this, and all is mended.
>
> (5.1.412–13)

Theseus's imagination has "amended" the Quince play by accepting it, listening to it, and not making fun of the actors to their faces. Its merit as a play consists in dramatizing his own social position and improving what we'd now call his "image" as a gracious prince. In itself the play has no merit, except in being unintentionally funny. And if it has no merit, it has no authority. A play that did have authority, and depended on a poet's imagination as well, would raise the question that Theseus's remark seems to deny: the question of the difference between plays by Peter Quince and plays by William Shakespeare. Theseus would recognize the difference, of course, but in its social context, as an offering for his attention and applause, a Shakespeare play would be in the same position as the Quince play. That indicates how limited Theseus's world is, in the long run, a fact symbolized by his not knowing how much of his behavior is guided by Oberon.

Which brings me to Bottom, the only mortal in the play who actually sees any of the fairies. One of the last things Bottom says in the play is rather puzzling: "the wall is down that parted their fathers." Apparently he means the wall separating the hostile families of Pyramus and Thisbe. This wall seems to have attracted attention: after Snout the tinker, taking the part of Wall, leaves the stage, Theseus says, according to the Folio: "Now is the morall downe between the two neighbours." The New Arden editor reads "mural down," and other editors simply change to "wall down." The Quarto, just to be helpful, reads "moon used." Wall and Moonshine between them certainly confuse an already confused play. One wonders if the wall between the two worlds of Theseus and Oberon, the wall that Theseus is so sure is firmly in place, doesn't throw a shadow on these remarks.

Anyway, Bottom wakes up along with the lovers and makes one of the most extraordinary speeches in Shakespeare, which includes a very scrambled but still recognizable echo from the New Testament, and finally says he will get Peter Quince to write a ballad of his dream, and "it shall be called Bottom's Dream, because it hath no bottom." Like most of what Bottom says, this is absurd; like many absurdities in Shakespeare, it makes a lot of sense. Bottom does not know that he is anticipating by three centuries a remark of Freud: "every dream has a point at which it is unfathomable; a link, as it were, with the unknown." When we come to *King Lear*, we shall suspect that it takes a madman to see into the heart of tragedy, and perhaps it takes a fool or clown, who habitually breathes the atmosphere of absurdity and paradox, to see into the heart of comedy. "Man," says Bottom, "is but an ass, if he go about to expound this dream." But it was Bottom the ass who had the dream, not Bottom the weaver, who is already forgetting it. He will never see his Titania again, nor even remember that she had once loved him, or doted on him, to use Friar Laurence's distinction. But he has been closer to the centre of this wonderful and mysterious play than any other of its characters, and it no longer matters that Puck thinks him a fool or that Titania loathes his asinine face.

Chronology

1564	William Shakespeare born at Stratford-on-Avon to John Shakespeare, a butcher, and Mary Arden. He is baptized on April 26.
1582	Marries Anne Hathaway in November.
1583	Daughter Susanna born, baptized on May 26.
1585	Twins Hamnet and Judith born, baptized on February 2.
1588–90	Sometime during these years, Shakespeare goes to London, without family. First plays performed in London.
1590–92	*The Comedy of Errors*, the three parts of *Henry VI*.
1593–94	Publication of *Venus and Adonis* and *The Rape of Lucrece*, both dedicated to the Earl of Southampton. Shakespeare becomes a sharer in the Lord Chamberlain's company of actors. *The Taming of the Shrew, The Two Gentlemen of Verona, Richard III*.
1595–97	*Romeo and Juliet, Richard II, King John, A Midsummer Night's Dream, Love's Labor's Lost*.
1596	Son Hamnet dies. Grant of arms to father.
1597	*The Merchant of Venice, Henry IV, Part 1*. Purchases New Place in Stratford.
1598–1600	*Henry IV, Part 2, As You Like It, Much Ado about Nothing, Twelfth Night, The Merry Wives of Windsor, Henry V*, and *Julius Caesar*. Moves his company to the new Globe Theatre.
1601	*Hamlet*. Shakespeare's father dies, buried on September 8.
1603	Death of Queen Elizabeth; James VI of Scotland becomes James I of England; Shakespeare's company becomes the King's Men.
1603–4	*All's Well That Ends Well, Measure for Measure, Othello*.
1605–6	*King Lear, Macbeth*.

133

1607	Marriage of daughter Susanna on June 5.
1607–8	*Timon of Athens, Antony and Cleopatra, Pericles.*
1608	Shakespeare's mother dies, buried on September 9.
1609	*Cymbeline,* publication of sonnets. Shakespeare's company purchases Blackfriars Theatre.
1610–11	*The Winter's Tale, The Tempest.* Shakespeare retires to Stratford.
1616	Marriage of daughter Judith on February 10. Shakespeare dies at Stratford on April 23.
1623	Publication of the Folio edition of Shakespeare's plays.

Contributors

HAROLD BLOOM, Sterling Professor of the Humanities at Yale University, is the author of *The Anxiety of Influence, Poetry and Repression,* and many other volumes of literary criticism. His forthcoming study, *Freud: Transference and Authority,* attempts a full-scale reading of all of Freud's major writings. A MacArthur Prize Fellow, he is general editor of five series of literary criticism published by Chelsea House.

ANNE BARTON is Professor of English at Cambridge University. She is the author of *Shakespeare and the Idea of the Play* and *Ben Jonson, Dramatist* as well as one of the editors of The Riverside Shakespeare.

RENÉ GIRARD is University Professor of the Humanities at Stanford University. His books include *Mensonge romantique et vérité romanesque (Deceit, Desire and the Novel)* and *La violence et le sacré (Violence and the Sacred).*

ALVIN B. KERNAN is Mellon Professor of the Humanities at Princeton University. His books include *The Plot of Satire, The Imaginary Library,* and *The Playwright as Magician: Shakespeare's Image of the Poet in the English Public Theater.*

RUTH NEVO is Professor of English at the Hebrew University of Jerusalem. She is the author of *The Dial of Virtue* and *Comic Transformations in Shakespeare.*

JAN KOTT is on the faculty of the State University of New York, Stony Brook. His drama reviews and essays written while he taught literature in his native country at the University of Warsaw are collected in the *Theatre Notebook.* He is the author of *The Eating of the Gods,* a study of Greek tragedy, and *Shakespeare Our Contemporary.*

DAVID MARSHALL is Assistant Professor of Comparative Literature at

Yale University. He is the author of *The Figure of Theater: Shaftesbury, Defoe, Adam Smith, and George Eliot.*

Northrop Frye is University Professor at the University of Toronto. His major books include *Fearful Symmetry, Anatomy of Criticism,* and *The Great Code.*

Bibliography

Allen, John A. "Bottom and Titania." *Shakespeare Quarterly* 18 (1967): 107–17.

Arthos, John. *The Art of Shakespeare*. New York: Barnes & Noble, 1964.

Barber, C.L. *Shakespeare's Festive Comedy: A Study of Dramatic Form and Its Relation to Social Custom*. Princeton: Princeton Uinversity Press, 1959.

Barton, Anne (Anne Righter). *Shakespeare and the Idea of a Play*. 1962. Reprint. Harmondsworth: Penguin, 1967.

Bellringer, Alan W. "The Act of Change in *A Midsummer Night's Dream*." *English Studies* 64 (1983): 201–17.

Berry, Ralph. "No Exit from Arden." *The Modern Language Review* 66 (1971): 11–20.

Bethurum, Dorothy. "Shakespeare's Comment on Mediaeval Romance in *Midsummer-Night's Dream*." *MLN* 60 (1945): 85–94.

Bonnard, Georges A. "Shakespeare's Purpose in *Midsummer-Night's Dream*." *Silliman Journal* 92 (1956): 268–79.

Bradbrook, M.C. *The Growth and Structure of Elizabethan Comedy*. London: Chatto & Windus, 1962.

Braddy, Haldeen. "Shakespeare's Puck and Froissart's Orthon." *Shakespeare Quarterly* 7 (1956): 276–80.

Briggs, Katherine M. *The Anatomy of Puck: An Examination of Fairy Beliefs among Shakespeare's Contemporaries and His Immediate Successors*. London: Routledge & Kegan Paul, 1959.

———. *Pale Hecate's Team: An Examination of the Beliefs on Witchcraft and Magic among Shakespeare's Contemporaries and His Immediate Successors*. London: Routledge & Kegan Paul, 1962.

Brower, Reuben A. *The Fields of Light: An Experiment in Critical Reading*. New York: Oxford University Press, 1951.

Brown, John Russell. *Shakespeare and His Contemporaries*. 2d ed. London: Methuen, 1962.

Bryant, Joseph Allen. *Hippolyta's View: Some Christian Aspects of Shakespeare's Plays*. Lexington: University of Kentucky Press, 1961.

Calderwood, James L. "*A Midsummer Night's Dream*: The Illusion of Drama." *Modern Language Quarterly* 26 (1965): 507–15.

Campbell, Oscar J. *Shakespeare's Satire*. 1943. Reprint. New York: Gordian, 1971.

Carroll, William C. *The Metamorphoses of Shakespearean Comedy.* Princeton: Princeton University Press, 1985.

Chambers, E. K. *Shakespeare: A Survey.* New York: Hill & Wang, 1958.

Champion, Larry S. *Evolution of Shakespeare's Comedy: A Study in Dramatic Perspective.* Cambridge: Harvard University Press, 1970.

Clayton, Thomas. " 'Fie What a Question's that If Thou Wert Near a Lewd Interpreter': The Wall Scene in *A Midsummer Night's Dream.*" *Shakespeare Studies* 7 (1974): 101–13.

Clemen, Wolfgang. *The Development of Shakespeare's Imagery.* 2d ed. London: Methuen, 1977.

Coghill, Nevill. "The Basis of Shakespearean Comedy." *Essays and Studies by Members of the English Association* 36 (1950): 1–28.

Colie, Rosalie. *Shakespeare's Living Art.* Princeton: Princeton University Press, 1974.

Cox, Richard H. "Shakespeare: Poetic Understanding and Comic Action (A Weaver's Dream)." In *The Artist and Political Vision,* edited by Benjamin Barber and Michael McGrath, 165–92. New Brunswick: Transaction, 1982.

Craig, Hardin. *The Enchanted Glass: The Elizabethan Mind in Literature.* Oxford: Basil Blackwell, 1950.

Dauenhauer, Bernard. "Authors, Audiences, and Texts." *Human Studies* 5 (1982): 137–46.

Dent, Robert W. "Imagination in *A Midsummer Night's Dream.*" *Shakespeare Quarterly* 15 (1964): 115–29.

Doran, Madeleine. "Titania's Wood." *Rice University Studies* 60 (1974): 55–70.

Draper, John W. "The Date of *A Midsummer Night's Dream.*" *MLN* 53 (1938): 266–68.

Eddy, Darlene Mathis. "The Poet's Eye: Some Shakespearean Reflection." *Ball State University Forum* 16 (1975): 3–11.

Edwards, Philip. *Shakespeare and the Confines of Art.* London: Methuen, 1968.

———. "Shakespeare's Romances: 1900–1957." *Shakespeare Survey* 2 (1958): 1–18.

Empson, William. *Essays on Shakespeare.* Cambridge: Cambridge University Press, 1986.

Evans, Bertrand. *Shakespeare's Comedies.* Oxford: Clarendon, 1960.

Faber, M. D. "Hermia's Dream: Royal Road to *A Midsummer Night's Dream.*" *Literature and Psychology* 22 (1972): 179–90.

Felperin, Howard. *Shakespearean Romance.* Princeton: Princeton University Press, 1972.

Fender, Stephen. *Shakespeare:* A Midsummer Night's Dream. London: Arnold, 1968.

Fergusson, Francis. *Shakespeare: The Pattern in His Carpet.* New York: Delacorte, 1958.

Fisher, Peter F. "The Argument of *A Midsummer Night's Dream.*" *Shakespeare Quarterly* 8 (1957): 307–10.

Foakes, F. A. *Shakespeare: The Dark Comedies to the Last Plays—From Satire to Celebration.* Charlottesville: University Press of Virginia, 1971.

Frye, Northrop. *Anatomy of Criticism.* Princeton: Princeton University Press, 1957.

———. "The Argument of Comedy." In *English Institute Essays (1948),* edited by D. A. Robertson, 58–73. New York: Columbia University Press, 1949.

——. *A Natural Perspective: The Development of Shakespearean Comedy and Romance.* 1955. Reprint. New York: Harcourt, Brace & World, 1965.

——. *The Secular Scripture: A Study of the Structure of Romance.* Cambridge: Harvard University Press, 1976.

Garber, Marjorie B. *Dream in Shakespeare: From Metaphor to Metamorphosis.* New Haven: Yale University Press, 1974.

Generosa, Sister M. "Apuleius and *A Midsummer Night's Dream:* Analogue or Source, Which?" *Studies in Philology* 42 (1945): 198–204.

Gesner, Carol. *Shakespeare and the Greek Romance.* Lexington: University Press of Kentucky, 1970.

Goddard, Harold C. *The Meaning of Shakespeare.* Chicago: The University of Chicago Press, 1951.

Goldstein, Melvin. "Identity Crises in a Midsummer Nightmare: Comedy as Terror in Disguise." *Psychology Review* 60 (1973): 169–204.

Granville-Barker, Harley. *Prefaces to Shakespeare.* 2 vols. Princeton: Princeton University Press, 1946–1947.

Green, Roger Lancelyn. "Shakespeare and the Fairies." *Folklore* 73 (1962): 89–103.

Greenfield, Thelma N. "*A Midsummer Night's Dream* and *The Praise of Folly.*" *Comparative Literature* 20 (1968): 236–44.

Greer, Germaine. "Love and the Law." In *Politics, Power, and Shakespeare,* edited by Frances McNeely Leonard, 29–45. Arlington: Texas Humanities Resource Center, University of Texas at Arlington Library, 1981.

Gui, Weston A. "Bottom's Dream." *American Imago* 9 (1952): 251–305.

Guilhamet, Leon. "*A Midsummer Night's Dream* as the Imitation of an Action." *Studies in Literature* 15 (1975): 257–71.

Hartman, Vicki Shahly. "*A Midsummer Night's Dream:* A Gentle Concord to the Oedipal Problem." *American Imago* 40 (1983): 355–69.

Hartwig, Joan. *Shakespeare's Comic Vision.* Baton Rouge: Louisiana State University Press, 1972.

Hawkins, Harriett. "Fabulous Counterfeits: Dramatic Construction and Dramatic Perspectives in *The Spanish Tragedy, A Midsummer Night's Dream,* and *The Tempest.*" *Shakespeare Studies* 6 (1972): 51–65.

Hemingway, Samuel B. "The Relation of *A Midsummer Night's Dream* to *Romeo and Juliet.*" *MLN* 26 (1911): 78–80.

Henze, Richard. "*A Midsummer Night's Dream*: Analogous Image." *Shakespeare Studies* 7 (1974): 115–23.

Holland, Norman N. ed. *Psychoanalysis and Shakespeare.* New York: Octagon, 1976.

Homan, Sidney R. "The Single World of *A Midsummer Night's Dream.*" *Bucknell Review* 17 (1969): 72–84.

Hunter, G. K. *The Later Comedies.* London: Longmans, 1962.

Hunter, Robert G. *Shakespeare and the Comedy of Forgiveness.* New York: Columbia University Press, 1965.

Huston, J. Dennis. "Bottom Waking: Shakespeare's 'Most Rare Vision.' " *Studies in English Literature* 13 (1973): 208–22.

——. *Shakespeare's Comedies of Play.* London: Macmillan, 1981.

Isaacs, Neil D., and Jack E. Reese. "Dithyramb and Paean in *A Midsummer Night's Dream.*" *English Studies* 55 (1974): 351–57.

Kermode, Frank. *English Pastoral Poetry: From the Beginning to Marvell*. London: Harrap, 1952.

———. *William Shakespeare: The Final Plays*. London: Longmans, 1963.

Kirschbaum, Leo. *Character and Characterization in Shakespeare*. Detroit: Wayne State University Press, 1962.

Knight, G. Wilson. *The Shakespearan Tempest*. 1962. Reprint. London: Methuen, 1971.

Kott, Jan. *Shakespeare Our Contemporary*. 1964. Reprint. New York: Norton, 1974.

Lamb, M. E. "*A Midsummer Night's Dream*: The Myth of Theseus and the Minotaur." *Texas Studies in Literature and Language* 21 (1979): 478–91.

Latham, Minor White. *The Elizabethan Fairies: The Fairies of Folklore and the Fairies of Shakespeare*. New York: Columbia University Press, 1930.

Law, R. A. "The Preconceived Pattern of *A Midsummer Night's Dream*." *Texas Studies in English* 22 (1943): 5–14.

Lawrence, W. W. *Shakespeare's Problem Comedies*. 1937. Reprint. Hammondsworth and Baltimore: Penguin, 1969.

Levin, Harry. *The Myth of the Golden Age in the Renaissance*. Bloomington: Indiana University Press, 1969.

McCary, W. Thomas. *Friends and Lovers: The Phenomenology of Desire in Shakespearean Comedy*. New York: Columbia University Press, 1985.

McFarland, Thomas. *Shakespeare's Pastoral Comedy*. Chapel Hill: University of North Carolina Press, 1972.

McPeek, James A. S. "The Psyche Myth and *A Midsummer Night's Dream*." *Shakespeare Quarterly* 83 (1972): 69–79.

Marcus, Mordecai. "*A Midsummer Night's Dream*: The Dialectic of Eros-Thanatos." *American Imago* 38 (1981): 269–78.

Mebane, John S. "Structure, Source, and Meaning in *A Midsummer Night's Dream*." *Texas Studies in Literature and Language* 24 (1982): 255–70.

Merchant, W. Moelwyn. "*A Midsummer Night's Dream*: A Visual Re-creation." In *Early Shakespeare*. Stratford-Upon-Avon-Studies 3, New York: St. Martin's, 1961.

Miller, Donald C. "Titania and the Changeling." *English Studies* 22 (1940): 66–70.

Miller, Raeburn. "The Persons of Moonshine: *A Midsummer Night's Dream* and the 'Disfigurement' of Realties." In *Explorations of Literature,* edited by Rima Drell Reck. Baton Rouge: Louisiana State University Press, 1966.

Miller, Ronald F. "*A Midsummer Night's Dream*: The Fairies, Bottom, and the Mystery of Things." *Shakespeare Quarterly* 26 (1975): 254–68.

Muir, Kenneth. "Pyramus and Thisbe: A Study in Shakespeare's Method." *Shakespeare Quarterly* 5 (1954): 141–53.

———, ed. *Shakespeare, The Comedies: A Collection of Critical Essays*. Englewood Cliffs, N.J.: Prentice-Hall, 1965.

Nelson, Thomas Allen. *Shakespeare's Comic Theory: A Study of Art and Artifice in the Last Plays*. The Hague: Mouton, 1972.

Nemerov, Howard. "The Marriage of Theseus and Hippolyta." *Kenyon Review* 18, no. 4 (1956): 633–41.

Olson, Paul A. "*A Midsummer Night's Dream* and the Meaning of Court Marriage." *ELH* 24, no. 2 (1957): 95–119.

Ormerod, David. "*A Midsummer Night's Dream*: The Monster in the Labyrinth." *Shakespeare Studies* 2 (1978): 39–52.

Parrott, Thomas Marc. *Shakespearean Comedy*. New York: Oxford University Press, 1949.

Pearson, D'Orsay W. " 'Vnkinde' Theseus: A Study in Renaissance Mythography." *English Literary Renaissance* 4 (1974): 276–98.

Peterson, Douglas L. *Time, Tide, and Tempest*. San Marino, Calif.: Huntington Library, 1973.

Pettet, E.C. *Shakespeare and the Romance Tradition*. 1949. Reprint. London: Methuen, 1970.

Phialas, Peter. *Shakespeare's Romantic Comedies: The Development of Their Form and Meaning*. Chapel Hill: University of North Carolina Press, 1966.

Poirier, Michel. "Sidney's Influence upon *A Midsummer Night's Dream*." *Studies in Philology* 44 (1947): 483–89.

Reynolds, Lou A., and Paul Sawyer. "Folk Medicine and the Four Fairies of *A Midsummer Night's Dream*." *Shakespeare Quarterly* 10 (1959): 513–21.

Robinson, J. W. "Palpable Hot Ice: Dramatic Burlesque in *A Midsummer Night's Dream*." *Studies in Philology* 61 (1964): 192–204.

Robinson, James E. "The Ritual and Rhetoric of *A Midsummer Night's Dream*." *PMLA* 83 (1968): 380–91.

Schanzer, Ernest. "The Central Theme of *A Midsummer Night's Dream*." *University of Toronto Quarterly* 20 (1951): 233–38.

―――. "The Moon and the Fairies in *A Midsummer Night's Dream*." *University of Toronto Quarterly* 24 (1955): 234–46.

―――. *The Problem Plays of Shakespeare*. New York: Schocken, 1963.

Siegel, Paul N. "*A Midsummer Night's Dream* and the Wedding Guests." *Shakespeare Quarterly* 4 (1953): 139–44.

Smith, Hallet. *Shakespeare's Romances: A Study of Some Ways of the Imagination*. San Marino, Calif.: Huntington Library, 1972.

Staton, Walter F., Jr. "Ovidian Elements in *A Midsummer Night's Dream*." *Huntington Library Quarterly* 26 (1963): 165–78.

Stoll, E. E. *Art and Artifice in Shakespeare*. New York: Barnes & Noble, 1951.

Taylor, Michael. "The Darker Purpose of *A Midsummer Night's Dream*." *Studies in English Literature* 9 (1969): 259–73.

Thomas, Sidney. "The Bad Weather in *A Midsummer Night's Dream*." *MLN* 64 (1949): 319–22.

Tillyard, E. M. W. *Shakespeare's Early Comedies*. Atlantic Highlands, N.J.: Humanities, 1983.

Toliver, Harold E. *Pastoral Forms and Attitudes*. Berkeley: University of California Press, 1971.

Turner, Robert K., Jr. "Printing Methods and Textual Problems in *A Midsummer Night's Dream*." *Shakespeare Bulletin* 15 (1962): 33–55.

Watkins, Ronald. *Moonlight at the Globe*. London: Joseph, 1946.

Weiner, Andrew D. " 'Multiformitie Uniforme': *A Midsummer Night's Dream*." *ELH* (1971): 329–49.

Welsford, Enid. *The Court Masque: A Study in the Relationship Between Poetry and Revels*." Cambridge: Cambridge University Press, 1927.

Wilson, John Dover. *Shakespeare's Happy Comedies*. Evanston, Ill.: Western University Press, 1962.

Wright, Celeste Turner. "The Amazons in English Literature." *Studies in Philology* 36 (1940): 433–56.

Young, David P. *Something of Great Constancy: The Art of* A Midsummer Night's Dream. New Haven: Yale University Press, 1966.

———. *The Heart's Forest: A Study of Shakespeare's Pastoral Plays*. New Haven: Yale University Press, 1972.

Zimbardo, Rose A. "Regeneration and Reconciliation in *A Midsummer Night's Dream*." *Shakespeare Studies* 6 (1972): 35–50.

Zitner, Sheldon. P. "The Worlds of *A Midsummer Night's Dream*." *South Atlantic Quarterly* 59 (1960): 397–403.

Acknowledgments

"The Synthesizing Impulse of *A Midsummer Night's Dream*" (originally entitled "Introduction") by Anne Barton from *The Riverside Shakespeare*, edited by G. Blakemore Evans et al., © 1974 by Houghton Mifflin Company. Reprinted by permission.

"Myth and Ritual in Shakespeare: *A Midsummer Night's Dream*" by René Girard from *Textual Strategies: Perspectives in Post-Structuralist Criticism*, edited by Josué V. Harari, © 1979 by Cornell University. Reprinted by permission of Cornell University Press and Methuen & Co. Ltd.

" 'A Little O'erparted': Actors and Audiences in *A Midsummer Night's Dream*" (originally entitled " 'A Little O'erparted': Actors and Audiences in *The Taming of the Shrew, Love's Labour's Lost, A Midsummer Night's Dream, 1 Henry IV*") by Alvin B. Kernan from *The Playwright as Magician: Shakespeare's Image of the Poet in the English Public Theatre* by Alvin B. Kernan, © 1979 by Yale University. Reprinted by permission of Yale University Press.

"Fancy's Images" by Ruth Nevo from *Comic Transformations in Shakespeare* by Ruth Nevo, © 1980 by Ruth Nevo. Reprinted by permission of Methuen & Co. Ltd.

"The Bottom Translation" by Jan Kott from *Assays: Critical Approaches to Medieval and Renaissance Texts*, (Volume 1), edited by Peggy A. Knapp and Michael A. Stugrin, © 1981 by the University of Pittsburgh Press. Reprinted by permission.

"Exchanging Visions: Reading *A Midsummer Night's Dream*" by David Marshall from *ELH* 49, no. 3 (Fall 1982), © 1982 by the Johns Hopkins University Press, Baltimore/London. Reprinted by permission.

"The Bottomless Dream" (originally entitled "*A Midsummer Night's Dream*") by Northrop Frye from *Northrop Frye on Shakespeare*, edited by Robert Sandler, © 1986 by Northrop Frye. Reprinted by permission of Fitzhenry & Whiteside and Yale University Press.